T0194592

"Success is subjective and best viewed as a journey. You will need strong desire to grow your expertise and network, develop the resilience and sharpen your instincts. These are intangibles with real-life principles laid out in Prove Yourself"- Aditya Humad, Co-Founder & CFO, The KICVentures Group

"This book is a potent initiator and energizer. It takes a simplified but holistic approach to success that will motivate and instigate."Dr. Kamilah Hylton, Dean Faculty of Science and Sport - University of Technology, Jamaica.

"Dr Chin grew up poor but dreamed big and believed that entrepreneurship was the way to incredible success, and Prove Yourself book outlines the keys for you to be successful in both business and life" – Dr. Jason Seale MBA, Medical doctor and healthcare entrepreneur.

"Prove Yourself detailed how Dr Chin's mother was crucial to his mindset to succeed and this reinforced my motivation to become the best version of me as an example to my daughter, so she learns to set her vision of who she wants to become and how to have an impactful, happy and grateful life." - Shweta Sharma, Director, R&D Program Lead, Biogen

"If you seek to rise in life, I strongly recommend you read this book to learn clues to guide your aspiration for financial and personal success. Prove Yourself is your toolkit for self-upliftment."
- Blake Brown, former deputy Head Boy of Kingston College and Chief of Staff of KIC Ventures Group Jamaica

Learn these twelve keys and follow clues from my journey to guide you to succeed in life and business.
Dr Kingsley R Chin, MD, MBA

A must read if you're a ….

High School Student
You are never too young to dream big. Start reading success books

College Student
Your leadership preparation starts to take shape in college. Read about my journey and start to think about yours

Parents
There is plenty of inspiring lessons on my journey from poverty to ivy league universities to becoming an orthopedic spine surgeon and ceo that you can draw lessons from to inspire your kids

Entrepreneurs
Books like this are necessary for you to read on how to succeed and follow the clues to success

Leader
Leaders learn from other leaders through study. This book provides the keys to first lead yourself and then apply to lead others.

This book takes you on a journey from the bottom of society to the very top of success in education, athletics, business, medicine, entertainment, philanthropy, leadership and family. You will ignite your desire to succeed and learn keys to prove yourself on your success journey.

TWELVE ESSENTIAL KEYS TO RISE IN
BUSINESS AND LIFE

PROVE YOURSELF
REVISED EDITION

KINGSLEY R. CHIN, MD, MBA

ARCHWAY
PUBLISHING

Archway Publishing books may be ordered through booksellers or by contacting:

Archway Publishing
1663 Liberty Drive
Bloomington, IN 47403
www.archwaypublishing.com
844-669-3957

ISBN: 978-1-6657-3899-6 (sc)
ISBN: 978-1-6657-3897-2 (hc)
ISBN: 978-1-6657-3898-9 (e)

Library of Congress Control Number: 2023902994

Print information available on the last page.

Archway Publishing rev. date: 3/15/2023

DEDICATION

I dedicate this book to serve forward all those who seek knowledge and inspiration to pursue a journey of unusual success in any areas of business and life. To my wife Vanessa and children Milan, Kingston and Blaze, you can always turn these pages to remind yourself of the lessons I lived. I am eternally grateful for the friends, family and colleagues who supported me through the many stages of my improbable success journey.

Kingsley R Chin, MD, MBA

CONTENTS

AUTHOR'S NOTE

When we decided to publish *Prove Yourself* in 2015, our company KIC Ventures, was the only Black-owned healthcare holding company in the world focused on investing in spine surgery. I was the Chief Executive Officer and had just recently celebrated the acquisition of Axiomed Corporation in 2014 with the world's most unique viscoelastic total disc replacement technology. The LESS Institute, my orthopedic and spine surgery clinical practice, was very busy treating patients with orthopedic and spine problems, and our medical device company, SpineFrontier Inc., saw sales rising year after year since 2007 with double digit EBIDTA. So in 2015 KIC Ventures was on track to generate over $40 million in combined revenues that year. My mindset was with all this rising success, I should publish a book that could help other entrepreneurs and the future generations of students who want to become entrepreneurs along with their parents especially single mothers like my mother. We published the book November 2015 and it turned out that many readers were inspired by my life lessons and self-development tips in addition to the concrete business start-up lessons. However, we also got suggestions to touch up the content and publish a paper back version. We also noted we were not getting student readers nor parents.

So we decided to publish a revised edition to add more about my life journey from childhood at the beginning of the book. We wanted students to see similarities with my struggles at all levels of my education. Can you develop a vision early in your childhood ? In this revised version the answer is yes, in fact you will see from my journey that I maintained my vision from early childhood to today. Most children dream big if presented with the environment and if they can then nurture the beginning of their vision it could be the guiding star for them the rest of their lives. This book should provide life inspiration for children.

I also added more insights into each chapter for readers who want in-depth easy-to-understand business lessons they can really follow. The original business lessons were expanded to be more usable in general and to be more easily digestible by anyone who want business literacy at any stages of life. Parents know students do not get financial lesson in their education even if they take business classes and so they will feel encouraged to find great lessons in this edition. The business financial lessons in this book are written to be easily applied not the academic form you get in business courses that are more business principles. It is my hope that readers can use the twelve lessons as a continuous reference in their every day life whether they are an entrepreneur now or thinking of getting a jump start on becoming an entrepreneur. I hope to see this book become a source of encouragement for entrepreneurship among young people in developing countries as the way to end world poverty and hunger and raise the standard of living for everyone.

At the end of the day, in this revised version of *Prove Yourself*, I further shared my life's journey and the twelve lessons that I followed to get started and navigated my way to what seemed like impossible personal and business successes for a poor Black boy born to a single teenage mother in a tiny town called Buff Bay, nestled along the North-East shores of Jamaica. If I could rise from poverty in a small country, dream and follow my dreams to attend the top Ivy-League Universities such as Columbia University, Harvard Medical School and Harvard Business School, plus build a successful company generating hundreds of millions in revenues and share my lessons for you to read, I expect you too will be inspired and feel bold to take on your own impossible journey after reading this book.

Let's go !!!

REFLECTIONS ON A PERSONAL JOURNEY

BUILD A PERSONAL STORY— DEVELOP A VISION

As long as I can remember, I have had the same vision. It is to be influential and impact the world. Notice there was no timeline attached to my vision. It was a journey to influence and impact without any measurement. Why did I have this big vision with no limits? How do you get such a big, limitless vision when you are a small boy growing up in Buff Bay, a small town on such a small Caribbean island as Jamaica? When I look back, I think it began with my father leaving my mother and setting in motion a desperate set of living conditions. When I realized my status in life, fatherless and poor, it created a powerful drive in me to succeed. When he abandoned me, my mother, and unborn sister to immigrate to London, England, to start a new life, I was barely one year old. I will never know if my life would have been better or worse had he stayed and raised me, and this is why I never blamed my father for leaving. Maybe I might have been too comfortable, or maybe I would have wanted to be like him instead of becoming myself. I was willing to be shapeless to learn from anyone and everyone and to become anyone I chose, with no one limiting me.

What about my mother staying with us? The fire in me to succeed might have been further set ablaze and my drive set in motion by my mother consistently guilting me, my younger sister, and two brothers by reminding us, had she not had us, she would have been more successful. This was her method of pushing us to aim and rise higher than she did and to avoid her mistakes, which limited her ability to rise higher in life.

At this point, growing up with a single parent in poverty in a small town, the odds of any of us succeeding were slim. The statistics for children raised by single mothers are dismal. More than 70 percent of incarcerated males were raised by single mothers. I was not aware of the odds stacked against me. I was too driven to succeed to even worry about odds. This is a lesson of success, to not limit yourself by others' expectations or the conditions you presently find yourself in. Life is not a race, so you don't need to compare yourself. Just run your own race to progress from where you start. God will put a drive in you that only you can feel and will create a vision that only you can really see. We all have a special life to live, and it is the personal feelings that determine what makes your life special.

DRIVEN BY POVERTY

I wanted no part of living in poverty, nor did I ever think of gaining money through crime. I was going to prove myself in life and rise to be financially successful and impact the world. Bill Gates was quoted as saying, "If we were born poor, it is our parents' fault, but if we die poor, it is our fault." I say it is nobody's fault for any part of your life that you want to change. I would rather be born poor and fight to be rich than be born rich and stay rich or, worse, die poor. We were very poor, and my mother was working six straight days a week, packing groceries in a supermarket to provide for us on a meager wage. Being the eldest meant that I received a lot of her attention, so she pushed me to get educated in school and in life but also whupped my butt for every action she thought could get me into trouble. Now I realize it was just her acting out of fear of something bad happening to me. I feel that fear with my own children today. Her methods included verbally scaring me with stories about the pitfalls of not getting educated and making bad life choices, starting with her own example when she had me as a teenager and had to drop out of school to work. Thank God for my grandmother, who helped raise us with love while my mother worked six straight days a week. From this experience, I learned the lesson to wait to have children until I am old enough and have achieved enough success so as to not have to sacrifice my future to struggle to raise children. It is different for women, due to the reproductive clock. Many women are claiming to be independent and deciding to not have children or wait until later in life when they find the right higher-valued man than themselves. This is risky since women might not have the right father ready when they are ready.

I had my first daughter, Milan, when I was forty-five years old. I credit my mother for initiating lessons on the importance of having key essentials to succeed, as I stuck to my plan to wait to have children until I was financially ready. This was an early lesson I had learned. Many, if not all, of the key lessons in these twelve chapters could be traced back to my journey to rise from poverty to life and business success. Lessons are critical for you to gain the knowledge to survive, succeed, and grow. I remember my mother had a brown chalkboard on the wall in the living room of our one-bedroom house, across from the sea and close to Lynch Park in Buff Bay, on which she would teach me about math and simple interest in saving money. Was this my first essential lesson on the value of money? At the time, no, but now I think it was a seed she planted in my head. So today, I expose my children to discussions on money early in their lives.

GETTING UP EARLY TO SUCCEED

My mother would be up at four o'clock every morning to make us breakfast so we could catch the earliest train to my high school in Port Antonio. I would walk across the football field at Lynch Park when it was still dark out to make it to the train station. Getting up at four is brutal for a child, but it was the only way to have breakfast and still make the 6:00 a.m. train. Here is another key essential that she taught me: get up early and prepare for your day to achieve. Today, I get up early like she did. Ideally, I get up at five or by six and get to the gym to work out, then go back to help my children prepare for school. I then start my day with scheduled conference calls to keep my mornings organized. Then I go to surgery or clinic to see patients if it is a day dedicated to patients; otherwise, it is all business. I travel every week for business.

KEEP LEARNING

My vision pulls me along and fuels my desire to continuously educate myself on how to succeed in life and business, to rise far above the low level that I started out at in life. How does my vision continue to drive me even though I have risen to much success? I have made it a habit to pursue success and to not become comfortable with past successes. The way you get success is from success, no matter how small. So I am always working on success, and as I achieve successes, I am able to see more opportunities to succeed. Daily, I look myself in the mirror to remind myself I am underachieving, and I must keep learning and staying relevant in the world today so I can make an impact and be influential. I know I can achieve more because when I compare what I know today versus a few months ago or a year ago, I see that I could have done better in the past if I had the knowledge I have today. You also don't know what you don't know you don't know, so I want to learn fast so I can achieve more. Achieving more is not just a quantity; for me, it is being able to win trophies and close out many of my opportunities. Many of my companies need to get to a point where they can be sold or go IPO. I look at other successful people and search for mistakes they make so I can learn to play better defense. If I can avoid mistakes before they happen or be ready to overcome mistakes, that is good defense.

I visit my mother in her humble home in Buff Bay and sleep there when I can, so I am reminded to be grateful and not forget where I started. I am blessed to have the talent and drive to pursue a vision far greater than anyone who grew up in my situation would be expected to have or would have imagined possible. I was the first in my entire family tree to go to college and to become an orthopedic and spine surgeon, or any kind of surgeon, so I don't know how far I can rise to, and the only way to find out is to keep rising. I am still the only orthopedic spine surgeon to grow up in Portland, Jamaica, and attend my high school. This is not an accomplishment I am proud of; it is more of a reality check on how much I am blessed. It is crazy to think I rose to go to Ivy League schools like Columbia University and Harvard Medical School and Harvard Business School. Therefore, it is my mission to go as far as I can get. To succeed, I know that every day I need to learn and improve. This is why I hope young children and readers of all ages read this book to learn key essentials from my journey on how I rose in life and business, to add to their own lessons and experiences to go as far as they can get in life and business. When you have a vision and you develop the daily habits that keep you on the path to succeed toward your vision, and you learn the key essentials to get success after success, then you will keep rising from level to level. I use the word *habit*, but it feels more like a process now, as I can scale up to take on bigger and bigger goals and apply the essential lessons, such as the twelve in this book, to get results consistently. Then my confidence level is high to start new projects and set new goals, but so too is my ability to pick the right ending before I start.

DECIDE WHERE YOU WANT TO GO
BEFORE YOU START THE JOURNEY

Anyone can dream up an idea and start it, but are you prepared for the journey? Do you have a sense of where you are going? Is the vision for your journey large enough to force you to keep going, never really getting to an end? I don't have a vision of the end of my journey, but I have visions of different mileposts along the way that act as lighthouses to keep me going and keep me away from ending in disaster, crashed up against the rocks, with the waves drowning me. When I start a journey, it is a process in which I apply the right strategies along the path, step by step, making adjustments as I go, but the journey I choose must be tied to my competence: what am I great at and as an expert? I know I must always be learning quickly and developing new skills or finding the right people to be around who can help me along.

When I look in the mirror, my reflection shows me that I am changing rapidly and reminds me that I am aging, so I must appreciate the value of time and also invest time in my health to prepare my body and mind to be healthy to work long hours each day and make time for my family and business team. As long as you are healthy and you use your time wisely and efficiently, you will create many opportunities to succeed and recover when you fail. We never know if we will get more than one opportunity to do something great, so I identify opportunities and make use of them, never taking for granted that I will get another one. I would take health and time over money any day. I remind myself that if you have a lot of money but no time, you are poor. So I am grateful that I have created businesses that allow me to control how I invest my time.

One reflection remains unchanged, and that is my insatiable and powerful drive to prove myself at every level. Leveling up is consistent for me. I don't remember resting at any level, celebrating that I have arrived and that I have succeeded enough. I remind myself that all great people and rich people eventually die and are mostly forgotten, except for the legacy of institutions they built and the work they did to help others, so I dedicate myself to achieving both a legacy of building companies and work to help others through mentorship and sharing my time and money. There is no retiring for me I am too grateful for my blessings to think about taking it easy one day. I wish to live to be 100 years old and to continue working. I published a YouTube video on Usain Bolt retiring much too soon. He said he did not want to start losing and that training is hard. I think his best races were still ahead of him, but he had to learn to change and adapt as he got older, not to retire early.

Once you give up, you risk regret. So when I get to a level, I quickly assess the new competitors and prepare to compete to stay at that level, to learn to succeed at that level, and prepare to move to the next level. As early as I can remember, I thrived on competition. When I am in the game, it is to learn fast, develop a strategy to win, and never quit; it's the same traits I look for in winners when I am watching others in their game. I search for clues to improve my game because winners leave clues. Successful people leave clues and processes you can follow in your own area of expertise. You don't need to reinvent the success wheel; you just need to build a better or different, more innovative use for the wheel. It is crazy that I cannot just enjoy a sporting event or look at someone in a leadership position and not measure myself against their success to see how I can learn from their success. I am energized by the learning experience and the opportunity to implement what I learn in my success journey, in order to prove myself.

TO BE A SUCCESSFUL LEADER INVEST IN MAKING OTHERS INTO LEADERS

See why I am motivated to write this book? It is for readers like you to learn the essentials for success in these twelve chapters and prove yourself by succeeding over and over on your life journey toward your vision, becoming an effective leader. The more I can invest in younger people, the greater the chance for me to leave an impact. If I am truly committed to impact the world and be influential, then it makes sense to teach others, so that my impact lives beyond me, and my influence is on others as they go on to learn from me.

Many leaders believe leadership is about ambition, titles, and being in a position of power to be adored or get rich, so they focus on themselves leveraging power over others. For me to consider myself as a successful leader, I decided to invest in building a team of leaders and helping those on my team to be successful, not thinking of only my individual success and my team as just workers or followers. I focus on building the systems and processes and empower and train people to fit the system or recruit the right people. Wherever I find myself in leadership, this is the way I lead. Along the way, I hope that everyone who shares time with me feels they grew as leaders and that I built and modeled a culture and system for them to be empowered and free to use their time efficiently. I don't try to know my impact because it is not about a scorecard for me to pat myself on the back, nor is there an amount of impact I am shooting for. A farmer will know the potential of the planted seed when he sees the harvest, not by sitting there and watching the seed grow into a plant. He has to water and nurture the seed and let it grow on its own time, and God will determine how much that seed will produce. I measure my investment in others by thinking of how I can invest in them daily and align their growth with my growth. Some results are daily, while others require years of growth. I have had employees with me for more than ten years who are still learning and are learning more rapidly each new year than all the years combined before. So anyone who spends time with me is subjected to daily motivation on life and leadership success. I subscribe to the belief that true leaders must be learners and must build others into leaders, not into workers and followers.

PROVE YOURSELF EVERYDAY

What does it mean to *prove* yourself? It means to have a personal vision and to prove that you can achieve it. You don't have to prove yourself to anybody—just to yourself. My vision to be influential and impact the world is my *why*, and it is not in comparison to anyone else's success. I then look at my what, how, and where. My what is the mission to develop businesses to advance health technologies and make health care cost-effective and accessible to everyone, equally, across the world. I feel great sense of empathy for suffering. I believe when someone is sick, they are at their worst, and this has a negative impact on their ability to be productive and live their greatest life. An economy will be stronger if the health care system and the people are stronger. I have a tough time seeing any living, breathing creature suffer in pain. I mean all types of pain—physical, emotional, and others.

I think the worst kind of pain is ignorance. When you are ignorant, you cannot understand your life and the decisions you make, and often, you will die tragically and untimely from an avoidable mistake. Ignorance leads to many poor decisions, habits, and painful life circumstances. The world would be much richer and more innovative if everyone was provided a great education. My *what* helps fuel my desire, which is the first of the twelve key essentials to success in this book. Your *what* should be framed as a problem and business opportunity to solve, and it must be big enough to make you feel if you achieve your what, you will also achieve financial freedom. Note the pursuit of financial freedom should always be aligned with your what. I would bet that any big vision requires some level of financial necessity, so you will be driven to get financial resources.

This brings me to "How will I achieve my vision and mission to be influential and make an impact?" First, I have to lead myself, be disciplined, and always be in a learning mode. I have come to know that you attract wealth after you have worked on yourself to have wealthy traits in habits like self-discipline, focus, and knowledge. Next is to have the resources to build companies and teams to execute our vision, mission, purpose, goals, and down-to-the-minute tasks. I think of companies as ships on which you are the captain, and it is your responsibility to keep the ship afloat and moving, and each employee is a shipmate. So I want to lead by example for anyone who comes in contact with me, to instill a sense of confidence that they can rely on me. A goal of effective leadership is to build respect for your team and in return gain their respect. If someone shows you lack of respect, they should be removed from your team, and if you show them lack of respect, they should remove themselves.

Know yourself and what you stand for. Know your standards, and these should shine through for others to know you in the same way. I see myself as being family oriented, driven, disciplined, resilient, hardworking, confident, intelligent, credible, a visionary, fair, humble, caring, an active listener, and having integrity. These traits are what I desired and worked to acquire; they were not what I was handed at birth. I believe who you become is what you were made to become if you remain a good person throughout life. You always have the choice to do evil and change the outcome of your life. If you do good, you attract good people and good outcomes. You become a good person with your own uniqueness that will flourish. I am never satisfied that I have acquired enough of any of these traits since I was not born with a finite amount of any trait. As I seek success, some days are better than others, but I benchmark my progress by how satisfied I feel when I exercise these traits and acquire new ones.

I often measure my life success by those I attract who are good and add value to my journey and by those I recognize as no longer good for me, and I walk away toward peace. If you possess value or money, be prepared to attract thieves who will steal your time, value, and money. How do they do this? Watch out for romantic relationships, friendships, and bad business deals; they are thieves of your time. Progress is a series of addition and subtraction of people in your life as you learn who is who around you. I constructively criticize myself, like saying I am an underachiever and underdog in a positive motivational way, but I never criticize others. Nobody loves the sting of criticism, but I have learned to embrace criticism despite the sting. I think you should try to be your greatest critic to improve—and also your most avid cheerleader to support you through the tough times when no one else is cheering. Despite achieving a high degree of relative success from humble beginnings and having high standards for exhibiting leadership traits, I get satisfaction when I treat people as just a nice, fun, and dependable guy. This comes across as charm since people love a confident, pleasant person. It is easy for me to be nice to people, as I constantly remind myself that I am a lucky kid from Buff Bay, Portland, Jamaica, who overcame great odds but never forgot his roots.

The where is global, but it began when I started to have small successes in my birthplace of Jamaica. I look forward to the success vision for Kingsley Investment Company (KIC) to have at least one of its subsidiaries as a public company in the USA by 2024. Looking beyond this goal, I hope to be in the position to help the United States of America and Jamaica in an impactful way, to pay my debt for all that both countries have given me. In order to make an impact, you need to have the desire, ability and resources at a minimum. Lucky for me, I am determined to grow and learn to become a transformational level 5 leader in order to take KICVentures Group, a KIC portfolio company, from good to great, culminating in its portfolio companies going public in the USA and building KICventures subsidiaries globally, starting in Kingston, Jamaica.

YOUR SUCCESS WILL BE OPPOSED BUT YOU MUST SURVIVE

With God's willing, I might be equipped to bring impactful leadership to Jamaica mostly in the form of investing capital to improve the economics of the country. I believe great leadership is portable. I would apply the same essential lessons for success in this book to lead any organization, public, private, or governmental. Additionally, I am learning from studying successful leaders of businesses, organizations, and countries to see what essentials they possessed or lacked, which I can learn from to make adjustments to achieve my vision. For example, I am a devoted student of Marcus Garvey and his belief that Black people need to pursue economic and political empowerment. He dared to think like an entrepreneur when he decided to buy ships to trade between Africa, the Caribbean, and the United States of America. This big dream scared the US government and the head of the FBI, Edgar Hoover, who called Marcus Garvey the most dangerous Black man in America. Imagine if Black men can come together to be entrepreneurial and industrious and dare to build enterprises. Seems the US government would be concerned with such a person like Marcus Garvey. Eventually, Hoover prevailed in prosecuting Marcus Garvey, claiming mail fraud for raising money from investors "improperly." Marcus was placed in prison, then deported to Jamaica, where he was ruined as a leader and jailed as he tried to rebuild his leadership stature. He left Jamaica broken and died in London a poor, broken man. Today he is the first national hero of Jamaica and adored worldwide for his legacy.

Mandela was deemed a threat and so was imprisoned by the South African government for twenty-seven years but was eventually released and became the first Black president of the country. Lee Quan Yew returned from studying in the United Kingdom to a poor and divided Singapore, but he was determined to transform the country. He showed the power of disciplined vision and intelligent transformational political leadership in daring to found the Political Action Party (PAP) and build Singapore into a first world economy. To do this, he decided to separate from Malaysia and tackle big problems between different ethnic groups and massive amounts of corruption. See how big vision and fearless determination can make you memorable?

We learn from these great leaders to think big and execute without fear of persecution. We are therefore building the business enterprises that could make us capitalized to invest in changing the American health care system and extending it to the Caribbean, Africa, and the world. To do this, I have leveraged my industry expertise in health care, technology, and information systems to create multiple companies under KICVentures Group.

TIME IS PRECISOUS BUT LIMITED

Every day, I feel like we are on borrowed time, and this creates the urgency for us to find revenues by getting investors, or sales, or a strategic merger or acquisition to have the money to grow our business and be strong enough to keep going despite opposition. I am quickly preparing the companies to attract leadership so they can go on without me. I have always worked on my succession plan for when I am to leave the company. I am willing to step down any day that I have a successor.In the meantime, the pressure forces me to elevate myself to a higher level of self-awareness and business prowess. Like Marcus Garvey, I feel the case to prosecute me is the greatest test I can imagine for an entrepreneur with a big vision.

My team and family are grateful for our lawyers and the fairness of the Massachusetts judge who presided over our arraignment, listened to the facts, decided to set me free on bail, and gave me my passport to travel to Jamaica to continue treating patients. I also get to give back philanthropically in my hometown of Buff Bay and parish of Portland. I took over the St. Georges Sports Club and football team and renamed them the Portlanders Sports Club and football club. I have poured millions of dollars and my time into improving the infrastructure at Lynch Park. As long as you are alive and able, I believe in giving your most to society and those whose lives you can help improve. I have also learned that as you transition to achieve great success, you will be challenged and tested to prepare you to transition to a higher level, and you will leave people behind who do not have the fortitude to go through the tough times with you to get to the next level. You need to develop the tough skin to handle greater levels of success. Your journey is to prepare you with hardship. The higher you rise, the more you are being watched as a Black man in America. This is supported by American history, so prepare to overcome; don't complain.

Each chapter in this book presents essential lessons on how

to prepare yourself as an organizational business leader. The same essentials can be applied to any organizational leadership position in business or your life. You are going to face many obstacles that will test you to the brink of complete failure. The first essential to depend on is your strong, unshakeable desire to succeed, which will be discussed in chapter 1.

LEARN FROM YOUR JOURNEY— MY HUMBLE BEGINNINGS

As a kid at Titchfield High School in Port Antonio, Portland, Jamaica, I used to be ashamed that our family was poor. I was ashamed I did not have a father. I was ashamed of the house we rented. When I took the bus from Port Antonio to my home in Buff Bay after school, I would not get off near my house. For a long time, I was determined to hide where I lived from the other kids I knew.

I remember dating a girl whose parents had returned from England and lived in Hope Bay, a small town east of Buff Bay. Things were going well until one day someone tipped her off that I lived in a poor house in Buff Bay. I laugh now, as I have had to learn that when you are succeeding, you will attract envy from people who are motivated to seek personal gain, so they sabotage your success. I still have people watching and hating on me, and there are those competing with me today, looking for ways to bury me through character and personal assassination and to then gain from my downfall, whether it is money or career advancement. Anyway, she approached me about it to see if it was true. I did not have to say much; she could smell the fear on me and knew the answer just from me standing there in shame. My brain was frozen. Before that moment, I had two strategies to avoid having to face my poverty: one was to have few close friends, and the second was to keep away from situations that would give away my secret—that I was dirt poor and ashamed. So I avoided dating girls in Buff Bay who knew my situation, but this was a new problem standing in front of me, waiting for a response. *What if the word gets around to girls who do not live in Buff Bay?* I went home that night in dread, and when I returned to school after that, I avoided her, and she avoided me. I stayed away from thinking about girls as a priority and focused on school and soccer. As the universe would have it, at fifteen years old, my problem of living in a small house was solved, and I went from living dirt poor to living in a white mansion with the head master of Titchfield High School, Mr. Lloyd O Chin, in the best neighborhood in Port Antonio and directly across from the high school. Wow, what a change! This is how the universe works even today; you really wish for something, and it will happen in due time, not on your time or exactly how you imagined it.

I had an interview with Ian Boyne on Television Jamaica (TVJ), in which I said, "When you are ready, your angel will appear." Appeared mine did. Now I did not have to hide where I lived, nor did I have to think about where I lived when talking to girls; they already knew. This did not mean I was no longer poor or suddenly became less humble. I kept a small circle of friends; that was never going to change just because my living situation improved. I liked moving by myself, and if I had friends, they would need to follow my lead and bring benefits, not kill my time on idle pursuits.

I move so quickly it is hard to maintain close friendships, as people are not me, so they have their own path and speed down that path. I was always trying to step up the quality of friends and girls that I would date in terms of people qualities, such as being smart, ambitious, humble, and genuine, to name a few. I teach my children to just be nice and kind.

Once I left Buff Bay and moved to Port Antonio, I never looked back. I was now in the capital city for my parish, Portland, and I needed to adjust fast and be ready to take advantage of the blessings my angel brought to me. This I did, and you can track many of the accomplishments that stemmed from this move as you follow my journey throughout this book.

Today, decide to accept your life as it is physically, mentally, emotionally, and financially. Then decide to start on your success journey. You can learn from mine by reading this book. You can start at any stage in life or at any age, and you don't have to finish since others can continue your journey. You are going to be happy if you want to get out of bed early every morning to work on your journey. Happy people have a sense of purpose every day. They give off positive energy and thus attract positive energy. Just be nice to people and see how nice they are in return. You can start at any age, in any place, as any gender, of any status, or in any circumstance. The important thing is that you start with a vision and build a desire to rise.

IMMIGRATING TO NEW YORK CITY AND COLUMBIA UNIVERISTY

I've always believed I was one of the poorest students to have entered an Ivy League university when I entered Columbia College in New York City. Maybe it was my shame coming back to me, like when I lived in Buff Bay. This was a negative thought, and negative thoughts will manifest in real life, but at that time, I did not realize how powerful my thoughts were, so I was lucky to have many more positive thoughts and goals than negative. When I got to Columbia College, I immediately got a job to support myself. I took a job in the John Jay student cafeteria. It seemed a brilliant idea. I got to eat for free and made money. I even started to make some friends with other students who worked there. All seemed great. School had just started, and as a freshman, it seemed all my friends were hooking up with girls either from the dorm or a class. I too made my first move.

I introduced myself to a girl from Long Island who I felt was a real gem. She was into me as well, fascinated by me being Jamaican. I asked her out on a first date to go to the movies. We picked a date, and game was on. I was on cloud nine. I was manifesting positive action and thinking, which landed me a date. What could go wrong? On the day we were supposed to go out on the date, I was working at the cafeteria when I noticed she was sitting at a table with her home girls. Here I was, working in the cafeteria in my baby blue and white uniform and white hat, working to be able to afford to take her out on a date. I couldn't hide, so I thought, *Let me go break the ice and show some confidence. After all, why should I be ashamed? I am a student and a top soccer recruit.* At this time, she knew nothing about my soccer abilities, but I did, so I had confidence. I went over, said hello, and introduced myself to her friends. This did not go over well by any stretch. These were girls from wealthy backgrounds, and my cafeteria job announced that I was not one of them. I cannot remember a word I said or that was exchanged; it was my numbing fear that left my brain frozen that I remember. I think I may have talked about our date coming up. The date never happened, and she gave me the complete brush-off in class the next time. It jolted me back to Buff Bay and Titchfield High School, so I went back to what worked. I focused again on school and soccer. This paid off big-time.

I got a big write-up in the school's newspaper, the *Columbia Spectator*, and that pushed up my prospects for dating. Once the season started, I blew up as a freshman starter on the varsity soccer team. I was a hot commodity, and my confidence level was high. This also meant I needed a more down-low job, so I took a job at the Columbia Library, working in the stacks. This allowed me to blend in with no uniform, and I could study on the job. I wished I could have been a fly on the wall when she realized that I was becoming the man. I don't remember her name, so I don't know what she did with her life, but she is highly likely to be successful. She was not meant to be with me, so no hard feelings; it is life. Maybe I should thank her for brushing me off to give me the drive and one more reason to develop my ferocious desire to rise above my start in life and learn the lesson to never put girls ahead of my ambition and vision.

I eventually settled with a wonderful girl who helped me with my work and who was super intelligent, ambitious, and beautiful and who appreciated me in every way. She would visit me in Jamaica on summer breaks, and I would visit her and her family in Kendall, Miami. She grew up around Jamaicans, including her best friend at Columbia, who was Jamaican. Plus her parents were from Trinidad, so we were an easy fit considering our shared Caribbean background. Eventually, we got married while we were in college. She graduated a year earlier than I did and went to Harvard Law School, where she graduated with honors and then came back to a very successful corporate law firm in Manhattan. As you read, you will learn that I eventually went to Harvard Medical School, but I started after she left Harvard Law School, so we were commuting between Boston and New York City.

Let's get back to where we left off. Enough about girls, as their female energy is a big distraction to your dreams if you are a guy, but I cannot seem to live without them, so girls are a constant thread throughout my life, as I love girls. A great girl in your life is a big asset but challenging to manage, and she is the greatest risk to your success and wealth. Back to the journey. So, whether I was the poorest student no longer mattered, but it did fuel my desire to prove myself and have others see me for who I was and not where I started in life. What mattered was that I began my journey to become influential and impact the world, and along the way, I made it into an Ivy League university and excelled while I was there—and you can do this and many more great things too, once you develop your vision and are eager to learn.

Just as I did, you will achieve the blessings to prove yourself and achieve tremendous success at every level along your journey. I can say I have realized some parts of my childhood vision to one day develop the skills to be an influential, effective, and caring leader, to provide jobs for people, to give back to my home country of Jamaica, to invest in young people, and to make an impact in this world with my many medical inventions—all while raising a family. I shower my children with love and pay attention to their growth to become successful in life, hopefully in ways that improve our world. My journey could be described as a miraculous rags-to-riches story. The humble start to my journey fueled my desire to develop my abilities and achieve great things. It was one way I dealt with the shame of my start in life. As I found success after success, I gained the means and access to resources that let me feel better about myself and instilled the confidence I needed to fully commit to rise above my start in life. I was setting even bigger goals, and my start in life began to feel like an advantage, an experience that made me feel different, and this feeling gave me the mindset to be driven and the belief that I was destined for big success. Today, I am prepared with the experience and education to be an effective leader of my family, people, and organizations at the highest level.

UNDERSTAND YOUR CHILDHOOD TO UNDERSTAND WHO YOU ARE

My journey to success began when I was born in the tiny seaside town of Buff Bay, in the parish of Portland, Jamaica, to a single, sixteen-year-old mother, Loleta L. Blythe. I was the eldest of four children. My father and namesake, Kingsley Richard Chin Sr., left for London, England, before I was one year old, to start a new life and a new family, and he never looked back to Jamaica. This sense of betrayal became a beacon to remind me to treasure everyone in my life who invested in me. Today, I vow to never give up on my children and birth country of Jamaica, thanks to my father's mistake. I have developed no tolerance for betrayal or disrespect, so I don't do either. My father made the mistake of giving up on

Jamaica and the blessing of watching my sister and me grow up to become successful adults. He missed the opportunity he could have had to share in all my successes and impact my life. My two sons and daughter, his grandchildren, have never seen him, so they don't speak of my father, and I do not bring him up. My father made his decisions and lived and then died with the consequences. He missed being a grandfather to my three children and died early in life from health problems and a broken heart. Time may have offered him the opportunity to make up, but he died too soon. This is a lesson for me and all fathers. Avoid becoming only a sperm donor father. Make things right at some point. You miss many opportunities to share in raising your offspring when you give up on being a father to your children. Time may run out on you to get a second chance.

Speaking of second chances, I would have gladly reconciled with my father at any point had he truly and sincerely tried to get back into my life to be a father. Maybe he just did not know how, and I did not prioritize reconciliation before he died. So it's never too late while you are alive to try to restore a relationship with your children. To any child or adult who is missing a parent in your life, try to reconcile with your parent while they are still alive. My father started the process for me to be born, so I thank him for that. Gratitude leads to forgiveness. Many men want to be fathers but are robbed of the opportunity due to bad blood between them and the mother of the child. This can be devastatingly painful for fathers who feel helpless and rejected and thus seek absence rather than face the pain every time they try to be there for their child. I advise any father in this situation to seek whatever legal help they can to get access to their children and fight to be there. Never give in or run away. My father did not experience this scenario. He left for England and chose to be out of sight and out of mind, but he had his reasons and faced the consequences. I cannot imagine that he did not have moments of regret, but he may have been too ashamed or pressured to return to Jamaica and be a father to my sister and me. The lesson is being a father or mother is more than a title; it's what nature intends to be the cycle of life, and children are a responsibility to continue life. Elon Musk is quoted as saying his kids did not choose to be born, so he owes them; they don't owe him."

The absence of my father drove me to have the essential desire early in life to succeed and one day fend for myself. I was blessed with athletic talents and a mother who was relentless at making sure I was focused on education. From a very early age, I wanted to make money to improve my situation. I admired my best friend's father, for he owned the largest wholesale business in Buff Bay and drove a large white car and lived in a beautiful house. My neighbor, who repatriated back to Jamaica, lived in as nice a house and was entrepreneurial. She asked me to sell frozen strawberry syrup mixture, or it could have been Kool-Aid in a plastic bag, at my primary school. I am guessing I was nine years old when I jumped at the opportunity. She also ran a truck that would go into the mountains to carry goods to the market in Buff Bay. Both were very short-lived experiences in early entrepreneurship, since my mother shut me down and made it clear that I must focus on education. I believe I became hooked on entrepreneurship, and this is why I believe entrepreneurs are made, not born. Expose your children to entrepreneurship early. For most parents, it is easier to invest in our children participating in school activities and sports after school and on the weekends but not expose them to entrepreneurship and money lessons.

My daughter Milan sold popsicles on the beach in Fort Lauderdale when she was seven years old. I have my kids watch YouTube videos in the mornings before school about how successful companies were founded and grew. They watch stories of billionaires and leaders of countries and companies. The goal is to plant seeds in children and hope they water them as they navigate through life. In my childhood, I took advantage of my talents and developed my athletic abilities across multiple sports while also being diligent in academics. My mother was only happy with my academic success, which I believe gave me the foundation to do well at everything else. There is some element of luck here, since many young children in similar situations do not have a mother to push them to get educated, and they may live in a country where the political leaders do not see children as an investment priority, so opportunities to develop as a child and advance in society are lacking or scarce if you are a poor child. It is difficult for single mothers to overcome the frustrations of poverty and broken romantic relationships to then show love and affection to their children. In fact, many single mothers abuse their children trying to discipline them, and these children feel unloved and resent their mothers. They easily get recruited into gangs and later become incarcerated in high percentages. My mother was strict about my education as the means for me to get a better life. If I were to give one piece of advice for success and stop writing here, it would be to be a learner and constantly seek to educate yourself, formally with degrees and informally by seeking mentors who give you work experience. I looked at the successful people in my community and decided I wanted to be successful, and the way to do so was to get an education. I started with a focus on formal education, and it still continues, but as I grew older, I put effort into self-learning, on-the-job training, and reading and studying successful leaders who I see as my mentors. The key is to keep learning so you can grow, seek opportunities, and be flexible in life and business to deal with the upturns and downturns. Learn from mentors alive and dead.

HIGH SCHOOL AT TITCHFIELD IN PORT ANTONIO, JAMAICA

As a young boy, I tried track and field, table tennis, cricket, and soccer. I quickly found that I was not fast enough to compete at track and field in Jamaica, which is legendary for sprinters, but I had enough speed to help me be relatively fast at soccer over short bursts.

I also gave up cricket because it was not going to get me to the US, where I believed I had the greatest opportunities for success. I gave up table tennis, but I played in high school. I was a member of the Titchfield High School table tennis team that won the national high school table tennis title against Kingston College in 1984. I lost my individual game, so it was bittersweet but satisfying to experience the team winning. Over time, I learned to appreciate that I made the team and tried to help win the trophy. I gave up table tennis and never played a competitive game after that tournament, as it was clear I had no future in competitive table tennis. After this reflection and process of elimination, I was left to focus 100 percent on soccer and be all in year-round. I had the same sense of focus on academics.

It was important for me to learn survival skills to get by, to learn from other people's mistakes and successes, to get along with others, to set goals that could help me get ahead in life, and to be flexible with my plans by playing the best cards I was dealt at every level. I felt very early on that being a great student and doing well at soccer was my ticket to getting scholarships to an American university, but it was still a very long shot, coming from a small school like Titchfield High School in a town as small as Port Antonio, a parish as remote as Portland, and a Caribbean country as Jamaica. The media focused on schools in the capital city of Kingston, so I had to excel and be different as a student-athlete to get the attention of the national media. I trained to become a prolific goal scorer, scoring as many as seven goals in one game my senior year in high school.

One of my most memorable games was against Calabar High School in Kingston on their home field, when they were being coached by Bradley Stewart, who was the current coach for the Jamaica Junior National Team. I was closely marked and ran out to the left side of the field just on the halfway line to receive a ball kicked high in the air from the goalkeeper. I trapped the ball on my chest and lobbed it over the head of my defender. I did this about three times, and by then I was across the field to the right and on top of the eighteen-yard line. I went horizontal with my left arm resting on the ground and volleyed the ball with my right foot into the right corner of the goal. I could see my coach, Donald Davis, and Bradley Stewart and many of the players and spectators cheering in appreciation. It was unusual moments like these that eventually gave me the success and media attention. When you dedicate yourself to achieving something, the universe will deliver if you do the preparation and wait for your angel to appear. I was rewarded with a starting position as center forward on the Jamaican Junior National Soccer Team for international competitions. This was the ultimate exposure and the break I needed to be one step away from going to the US on a scholarship. I later found out that Coach Stewart gave me a strong reference that would yield me a soccer scholarship to the United States. Amazing how hard work and patience pay off at the right time.

COLLEGE IN THE IVY LEAGUES AT COLUMBIA UNIVERSITY IN NEW YORK CITY

In 1984, I got the call to play varsity at the then number one university in soccer in the US, Columbia University in New York City. All my work and preparation were about to pay off big-time. Columbia was an Ivy League academic and soccer powerhouse. Columbia was ranked number one in the US at soccer, which meant I was among the top recruits in America. Columbia had been undefeated the previous year (1983) but lost in overtime to Indiana University in the finals, 1–0.

I took advantage of this scholarship opportunity academically and worked really hard to achieve as much success as I could while I was in college. I graduated with a dual degree that took me five years, a bachelor of science in electrical engineering and bachelor of arts in mathematics. I also held a membership in the prestigious Eta Kappa Nu Electrical Engineering Honor Society. Because I was in a special five-year dual bachelor's degree program, all my friends graduated and left me behind while I completed the extra fifth year. It was hard to see all my friends graduate and leave me behind, but I was focused on finishing the goal I had set to graduate with two degrees. I am not one to be afraid to go it alone. To be an exception, you have to make exceptional decisions to get exceptional results.

My high school soccer coach, Donald Davis, had spent time in the United States, where he graduated with a degree in psychology and played professionally for the New York Cosmos soccer team, alongside Pele, the greatest soccer player of all time. I listened and learned a lot from my coach. I recalled when he told me to make sure I earned my "paper" (degree) when I got to the US; unfortunately, many other Jamaican soccer players who had the chance to go to a US university on scholarship did not finish their degrees. Not only did I get my degrees, but I also was an academic honor society member and started my journey to leadership by being elected president of my senior class's student government, an honor that I treasure, being that it was the first time a black student had ever held this position throughout the Ivy League. Being the first Jamaican was good enough for me, but it was time to break that barrier and hope others would follow one day.

I also dedicated myself to soccer to help our team win two Ivy League championships, and I was ultimately voted by the coaches as player of the year in 1988. During college, I always held a work-study job—from the cafeteria to the library, to the gym, to working at the Columbia Journalism School, where I appreciated the power of the camera and media. Remember how I wanted to stay low-key in my jobs after that cafeteria embarrassment? I also worked outside the university for a summer at AT&T Bell Laboratories in Parsippany, New Jersey. At this point, I was thinking of building a career as an engineer. However, the experience did not energize me to continue as an engineer. Instead, I wanted to leverage my engineering education into business and Wall Street, which became a new target. It is a consistent trend for me to realize my situation and to change and go where my strengths will help me succeed to achieve my goals and improve myself. The lesson is to stay fluid to fail fast or start a new journey.

MY FIRST JOB WORKING IN MANHATTAN AND ON WALL STREET

After graduating Columbia, I got business experience working at Andersen Consulting (now rebranded Accenture) in its New York City office as an experienced IT management information systems consultant in the financial services sector. My first assignment was at Cigna Insurance Company in Hartford, Connecticut. Here I was exposed to health insurance as a business. Personally, it was an opportunity to also live among fellow Jamaicans, as there was a large concentrated Jamaican community in Hartford. I lived in Simsbury and Bloomfield. Next, I spent six months on assignment at Goldman Sachs on Wall Street, setting up their computerized portfolio management information system. This was my close encounter with Wall Street and the impact of organizational financial success and investment banking and the power of software to empower leadership decisions. Wall Street was a goal, and I had achieved it, so I was pumped to explore a career in business and investment banking. Working in New York City, however, quickly exposed feelings of insecurity and insignificance, as I was lost in the vast financial services machinery. I wanted to leave to move to the next level and one day return to New York City, after I had proven myself to be a significant player in business. So it was time for me to move on and leave the city. When I made this decision to leave New York City, my wife was about to graduate from Harvard Law School and so was interviewing for jobs in New York City. I was commuting in my red Honda Civic Hatchback from New York to Boston every weekend. I had paid $4,000 for a used car. It was my first car. This was a grueling trip, and I had to be intensely alert, as there were always state troopers camping out and roaming the highways. I was stressed about avoiding police as I drove the trip, which took three to four hours.

In three years, I never got stopped once by the police, so I felt that my strategies worked for me. I avoided the left lane, stayed in the middle lane, hid behind trucks, and never took the lead when driving fast. I would follow fast cars and stay enough behind to avoid being grouped in a speed trap. I was excited to have her return to New York, but this changed once I got accepted to Harvard Medical School and decided to go. I had to choose ambition over love and marriage, given my intense drive to succeed at my vision. My wife was very understanding, and we divorced amicably. She has since gone on to be a great lawyer in corporate America and academia.

MEDICAL SCHOOL AT HARVARD UNIVERSITY IN BOSTON, MASSACHUSETTS

How did it happen that I left New York City for Boston, Massachusetts, and Harvard Medical? I had to decide what my next move was. While I tried to figure it out, I looked into graduate school for engineering and business, and I looked into law school as well. I took entry examinations for each, as I kept changing my mind. One of my keys is that I stay in motion to try things out, while also doing research and gaining knowledge so I can make an informed decision. I finally settled on taking the MCAT for entry to medical school, thinking I would come back into health care or investment banking. I was accepted to every medical school I applied to. I narrowed my decision down to Yale and Harvard. After visiting the Harvard Medical School campus, it just felt clear to me that this was the best of the best, and I felt I belonged there. I was so lucky and blessed to have this opportunity to study where many of the greatest doctors and surgeons studied. I also felt this would be a significant milestone for other aspiring students to follow me and achieve. *Who would have imagined, seeing me as a little boy in Jamaica, that I would have risen to this level?* I thought. My wife and I sat down and discussed all the options. She could not appreciate why I would not stay in New York City at any of the really great medical schools. I knew I couldn't turn down Harvard Medical School, and I knew this meant I had to make a choice between her and Harvard. I chose Harvard, and we split.

I went to Boston and spent ten years at Harvard Medical School—four years in the medical school and six years at the Harvard hospitals in the Harvard Combined Orthopedic Residency Program (HCORP) (the most prestigious training program in the world to become an orthopedic surgeon).

My business exploits continued after I left New York City. While at Harvard Medical School, my interest in health care technology led me to found RemoteVitalsSign., software that was intended to allow doctors to have vital signs uploaded from the bedside to their Palm Pilot remotely, so they could have this information for rounding and managing their patients. This would solve the problem of manually writing down all the patient's vital signs on paper. I hit a roadblock in the software with collecting the urine output in real time and interfacing with different software that other hospitals used. This was an idea that was too soon, so I abandoned it but not my desire to build successful health care software. I felt health care software was lacking, but the need for efficiency was high and urgent. I value resilience, and I teach my kids to never quit. For quitting then be-comes an option, even a strategy, when faced with the smallest of obstacles. Resilience is getting stronger in your pursuit of success when you are faced with great challenges that should make you quit, but you don't quit; you bounce up even higher than where you were before you fell or were pushed down.

I then founded Meduwed, my second software company. This was a health care distance learning software company. I acquired Cognate, a java-based software company founded by two students who were studying computer science at Massachusetts Institute of Technology (MIT) in a deal worth $150,000 in cash and 12.5 percent of Meduweb. We were positioning this internet company in health care education distance learning when the dotcom bubble burst in October 2000. I made the mistake of abandoning yet another software company. I credit these failed experiences in changing me to act with urgency and perseverance. I made a big mistake here in that I did not commit to the internet as an opportunity. I am still angry at myself, and I take out this feeling today by being obsessed with being an industry leader in the business of spine surgery and health care information systems using internet social media tools. I was determined to start another software company and this time never quit.

My opportunity came when one of our team members sold us his heads-up display technology. I was sold on the concept of a heads-up display hardware gadget on your dashboard, holding your cell phone and projecting in front of the screen. I saw the growing power of the phone and the camera and believed the traditional dashboard would be replaced by a heads-up display that projected ahead. We debuted it at the 2015 Consumer Electronic Show (CES) in Las Vegas under the name SenseDriver Technologies.. It was a smash hit. People were excited to sit in our demo car and test the technology using voice control. We had insurance companies and car companies meet with us back at our home office. We, however, made a fatal mistake. We focused on building the hardware, and this took a long time and needed funding. We continued to develop the software under a new name SenseSay.. Eventually, the market for the heads-up display fizzled, and we were left with nothing. Rather than quit this time, we pivoted into looking at social media applications. We felt there was a gap in health care information sharing and that electronic medical records (EMR) should not be office based; instead, each patient should carry their own medical information and give providers access in a HIPPA-compliant and secured platform. I spent several hours a day studying social media on the major platforms, especially LinkedIn, Facebook, Instagram, Twitter, YouTube and WhatsApp. I am on TikTok but not as active yet as I am on LinkedIn or IG. The result is our team has invested in building Neetworkiin and Mediconnects, two collaborative, networking enterprise software companies determined to build digital engagement communities using social media tools. The timing was great for this when COVID-19 hit and people started to work remotely and spend more time on social media. Mediconnects is a social media platform dedicated to medical information and experience sharing while building a community. If we develop a digital engagement community, health care providers and insurers can get data directly from the point of service real time, and this data will guide cost savings and more effective preventive health measures. More sharing of information and experiences will make people more educated about their health and guide what products and services get adopted. Imagine if the world had Mediconnects when COVID-19 started in China? We could share information socially and track the disease before it became a pandemic. Instead, we relied on the news and government action, which kept us fearful and in the dark. Today, I push myself to study and execute quickly when the opportunity is there, because you never know how the market or an opportunity will change in an instant, and you need to change with it, not abandon your idea when faced with obstacles or challenging circumstances.

BECOMING A MILLIONAIRE: MAKING MY FIRST MILLION IN REAL ESTATE

Making my first million obviously made me a millionaire by definition, but I did not feel like I was a millionaire when I had a net worth of a million dollars. For one, I did not have a million dollars sitting in the bank. Second, I did not set out to become a millionaire with a clear timeline or finish line, so when I realized I had a million dollars in net worth, I was too busy working hard to keep building to stop and celebrate. This is an important lesson to share. I was a millionaire before I was a millionaire, since I had put into place the systems and business to become a millionaire, and I was thinking and acting like a millionaire before I had a million dollars. Here is what happened, so you can see that it was a journey, not a destination.

I believe I was prepared with the essentials to succeed at my next business venture. I needed to find a problem I could solve with a business and have the desire to pursue it no matter what obstacles I faced. It came to me when I moved out of the dorm at Harvard Medical School and into an apartment in Jamaica Plains. But why did I leave the dorm? Convenience. Being single and dating while in a medical school dormitory did not seem accepted. I couldn't keep my romantic life private when everyone wanted to meet any girl I brought to the dorm. This became too close for comfort, so I decided I needed my own private apartment, not just for dating but to feel I was living a normal life away from the other students who were in the dormitory. I was surprised by how cheap my rent was at the time. I looked at the amount of rent I was paying in the middle of a large city like Boston and compared it to what I was paying when I lived in New York City.

I decided that I would look into real estate as an opportunity. First, I would own an apartment rather than renting. I had an insight that real estate was going to go up to eventually match cities like New York City and San Francisco, with similar demographics. I thought I could own apartments and rent to students similar to myself. I leveraged my knowledge of the real estate market in New York City to realize that there was a problem with limited supply of real estate in Boston for an underserved niche that consisted of students and young graduates and people starting a family. How did I start? Well, I met a girl who was from Jamaica and came to Boston to study at Boston University. I knew her cousin well since we were roommates sharing an apartment in Jersey City before I went to Boston. I met her at her graduation. In short, we were married about eighteen months later. She was living in Cambridge, so I moved into her apartment to save on rent and to live together. I told her about my real estate vision. At the time, she had gotten into Northeastern University's master's in business administration program. We started to research the market and felt that with rent control just abolished in Cambridge, we had an opportunity to get cheaper real estate. Plus, students would love to live in Cambridge. So I targeted Cambridge, Massachusetts, where Harvard University and Massachusetts Institute of Technology were both located, just across the river from Boston University. We had about $2,000 in savings, and we borrowed another $8,000 to buy our first two-bedroom apartment. We established a system where we would buy at least two bedrooms with a deck and two parking spaces. It worked. We renovated the apartment and sold it six months later and made $100,000 in profits. I convinced her to become a real estate agent and source properties for us to target. We used the profits and bought real estate and built a real estate construction team that modernized properties in Cambridge, Massachusetts. I knew prices were much lower in Cambridge than in New York City, and I predicted that prices would rise. So I bought great properties at low prices, renovated them, and resold them at a higher price as the market heated up, which made me a millionaire many times over very quickly.

This was going great until I was faced with graduation and a year of additional training in spine surgery in Cleveland. This meant I had to leave Boston for at least a year, since I was not convinced I wanted to practice as a spine surgeon in Boston, and I wanted to get the best spine training. I never stopped thinking about my vision, so my desire was no less now that I had money. I had a discussion with my wife about leaving Boston, and she was OK but wanted me to come back to practice there so we could continue our real estate business. By now, I was doing more than real estate. I was always thinking about software. Plus, I did not feel the compelling desire to continue to run a real estate development company, even making millions doing it. Money was never a pursuit; it was influence and impact. The money will flow, as it is a cycle. Money is great but is not what motivated me. The process of making money building technologies in health care was more enticing. Had I kept up the real estate business, it would have made me millions and millions, but I don't believe I could have also focused on spine surgery, which I wanted to do, in addition to software development. I had to prioritize my passions. I vowed that I would come back to real estate when I had capital from my health care investments.

BECOMING AN ORTHOPEDIC AND SPINE SURGEON AT HARVARD MEDICAL SCHOOL

In 1996, I graduated with honors from Harvard Medical School. I was accepted into the Harvard Combined Orthopedic Residency Program (HCORP), and in 2002, I graduated as an orthopedic surgeon, with an added fellowship in adult reconstructive surgery. After graduating, I was accepted into the number one ranked spine fellowship in the country, located in Cleveland, Ohio. So I spent a

year in Cleveland, training with the renowned professor of orthopedics and spine surgery, Dr. Henry H. Bohlman, to specialize in
spine surgery.

Two weeks into my fellowship, Dr. Bohlman offered to hire
me into his practice. Initially, I was flattered and accepted, but
I later changed my mind. You can never fill a great man's shoes.
After Cleveland, I was offered the prestigious position as the chief
of spine surgery and assistant professor of orthopedic surgery at the
University of Pennsylvania Medical School in Philadelphia. Here I
was going to be able to fill my own shoes. The saying "opportunity
favors the prepared" really applied to this situation. Because I had
written more than twenty papers and book chapters and was coming from prestigious Ivy League academic programs, I was a serious
candidate to fill the job opening and be the chief of spine surgery
in an academic environment, where experience was not the only
requirement.

After I became chief of spine surgery, I wanted to remove any
doubt that I was the right candidate for the job, since I lacked the
expected ten years of experience, and I felt the pressure of being the
only Black spine surgeon and chief of spine surgery at a major academic institution, especially in the Ivy League. I worked very hard
to put together a curriculum for the residents, initiated a pipeline
of research publications, wrote my first textbook with Lippincott
Publishing, brought in the latest spine equipment, and connected
with the emergency ward to put protocols in place to manage spine
patients, among other initiatives. Needless to say, within a few
months, I felt the Division of Spine Surgery was strengthened, and
we hired a second spine surgeon a year later.

But what about my promise to my wife to return to Boston?
Well, she decided to move to Philadelphia, where we would apply the
same formula to allow us to run our real estate company. Again the
conditions favored us, since Philadelphia's real estate was substantially lower than New York City's, and we believed the prices would

also rise as they did in Boston. There were also lots of universities and businesses for students and young professionals who would want to own real estate. So we sold many of our units in Boston and bought up many condominiums in Philadelphia, and my wife joined a prestigious real estate firm working in the Rittenhouse Hotel in the heart of Rittenhouse Square and Philadelphia.

We bought three adjoining condominiums in the Wannamaker House on the seventeenth floor, with amazing views at the corner of Twentieth and Walnut Street, a stone's throw from my new job at the University of Pennsylvania Medical School as an assistant professor of orthopedics and spine surgery. We bought several other units, which we rented out. The compromise worked for my wife, as she picked up right where she left off in Boston, but the market was new, so she had to work hard to build her client list. The decisions I made all set into motion new journeys.

FOUNDING KINGSLEY INVESTMENT COMPANY (KIC): OUR HEALTH CARE INVESTMENT PORTFOLIO HOLDING COMPANY

In 2000, I filed my first US patent application to improve lumbar spine surgery based on Dr. Art Steffe's pedicle screw-based plate fixation idea. I thought using Steffee plates in an X-shaped configuration would allow for segmental fixation both for fusion and for dynamic stability. This was the founding idea that led to Kingsley Investment Company (KIC), our parent health care investment holding company to develop patented health care technologies and other businesses to solve problems in spine surgery. My second patent application was for a total lamina and facet replacement, an idea I got while sitting in a lecture on facet replacement by Dr. Mark Reiley, the founder of Archus, a facet replacement company, at a spine conference as a resident. I was hooked on spine surgery and the idea of finding technologies that could replace the facets. I next developed a concept for a minimally invasive percutaneous pedicle screw system I later called the minimal access nontraumatic insertion system (MANTIS). The idea for MANTIS came out of the need for new and innovative percutaneous pedicle screw systems, and many companies were lacking one to compete against Dr. Kevin Foley's and Medtronic's Sextant. In 2004, I decided to develop the MANTIS into a product and form a company for it. The following year, 2005, while in Philadelphia, I incorporated KIC as the holding company with the first portfolio company MANTIS LLS. We sold the MANTIS along with its assets in a multimillion-dollar deal to Stryker Spine, a publicly traded company and a leader in orthopedic medical devices. In sports analogy, I had won a championship ring and now was among the small group of elite surgeon entrepreneurs with a similar accomplishment.

I learned from this experience and was now thinking of how we could replicate the MANTIS and start other companies to innovate and commercialize on the global stage rather than just developing a single device in its early stage for sale to a larger company. This led to the formation of SpineFrontier LLS in 2006. We had a concept for another percutaneous pedicle screw system called the MISquito. While selling the MANTIS, we declined an offer from Zimmer Spine, so I felt we could sell them on the MISquito as better than the MANTIS. However, this time around, I chose to do it on my own by partnering with other spine surgeons to develop the concept further and bring it to market.

This was about the time I met a former Bohlman spine fellow and surgeon. He was a big Zimmer user, especially their trabeculae metal cervical cage, so I felt he could help me get a meeting with Zimmer. He liked the idea of the MISquito and decided to invest $1 million in SpineFrontier with me. Once he invested, he introduced me to other spine surgeons who also invested and formed our strategic advisory board (SAB). Minimum investment at the time was $500,000. Our SAB met in Montego Bay, Jamaica, to develop our mission statement and to kickstart the company with a commitment to work together. This led to many meetings to discuss strategies and product feedback for improvements. We also met to have cadaver demonstrations so we could get feedback on the devices and instruments. A common meeting place was in Providence, Rhode Island, at a training center. We met in Baltimore at another training center and also at our headquarters in Beverly, Massachusetts. We did not sell the MISquito as I thought we would. It was very hard to get to the C-suite to sell any device, and this started our journey of stumbling forward, as we had to learn how to do the basics of developing a concept and engineering it into a product, then manufacturing it and filing for FDA clearance before it could be commercialized. We had to learn how to design instruments to go with the device and new technique changes, which fed back into design changes. We had to rely on ourselves as founding surgeons to put in the time to learn from the competition what to develop. I was convinced that percutaneous surgery was the future, so we embarked on developing a facet screw system called FacetFuse. We developed the first multiaxial washer, which sat on the head of the facet screw rather than the traditional place for a washer, under the head of the screw. We designed the instruments to improve the technique, and it was the first design to allow placement of a screw in the spine using a power drill. We had to learn so much so much so quickly. We hjad great success with this product to the tune of over $5 million in annual sales our best year. In retrospect we should have sold that company or seek funding to grow the revneues further to make the company more attractive. The bigger companies were not looking to buy a facet screw eventhough we made the case that it was an effective solution and less invasive than pedicle screws. We found ourselves with no company to buy our products so we decided to focus on research and development with both a big "R" and a big "D" with less focus on sales. The goal was to develop nitch technology solutions and with time build the value for an initial public offering (IPO).

With so much focus needed for KIC and SpineFrontier, what about the real estate business which made me my first million? I decided to start Kingsley Real Estate Holding LLS under KIC. However, I also decided soon thereater to suspend my real estate business, with valuable knowledge and the confidence that I could do it bigger again in the future once I had more capital and the time to focus on real estate. Now it was time for me to focus on becoming a spine surgeon, on becoming the best spine surgeon, or at least a different kind of spine surgeon and applying my knowledge and expertise into advancing our medical device technologies. This was what I needed to focus on to achieve my big vision. My wife at the time disagreed with my desire to focus on health care investments instead of real estate, and we fought over the money and how we should use it. We ended up in a divorce. I remembered her saying she married a spine surgeon, not a businessman. She went back to Boston to continue the real estate business we left in Cambridge, and I went to West Palm Beach in South Florida to start a private academic practice called Institute for Minimally Invasive Spine Surgery (iMISS), to focus on less invasive spine surgery. This later became Institute for Modern and Innovative Spine Surgery, then changed to the Less Exposure Spine Surgery (LESS) Institute. Today, it is the LES Clinic with offices in Fort Lauderdale, Arizona, and Jamaica. I now had a bigger goal to vertically integrate the medical devices with a clinical practice umbrella and later add a software platform, initially called LESS Institute online (LESSi), with members insured online. LESSi has now morphed into Mediconnects Inc. If we could continue to get more surgeons to invest and partner with us, we could transform health care since we were closest to the problem and had an interest in developing the solutions for ourselves so we could treat patients more effectively.

The vision of thinking big is a sum of first getting small wins and having focus. With SpineFrontier Inc., we could use the lessons learned to build competitive medical devices focused on spine surgery. I felt we could do it better than Stryker, but it would take time and patience. Over time, we identified more growing problems we saw in spine surgery as a guide to develop innovative devices, instruments, and techniques. Our goal was to build best-in-class products in each problem area of spine surgery and look for problems elsewhere more broadly in orthopedics.

As we progressed, I saw the need in 2013 to build a venture arm to KIC we called KICVentures Inc., a wholly owned subsidiary of KIC, to be the investment vehicle through which we could develop a holding company with a comprehensive portfolio of companies focused on the spine but positioned to develop technology solutions to health care problems or acquire companies that already have solutions. We were just not going to do well growing revenues to become another big spine company. Rather, we would be better at developing innovative technologies or acquiring them and then looking to sell, go public, or license the technologies to generate revenues and ultimately take the parent company, KICVentures, public. This was a radical change for our employees and investors from the SpineFrontier R and D model. It took several years to transition from SpineFrontier to KICVentures. With KICVentures, we acquired AxioMed Corporation and all its assets in 2014, because of their innovative viscoelastic disc replacement for the cervical and lumbar spine. This was a complementary technology platform to SpineFrontier's minimally invasive fusion platform, but we kept AxioMed separate as its own company with employees and a quality system and manufacturing. Today, we changed the name KICVentures to KICVentures Group Inc., as we have many portfolio companies with diverse products. AxioMed really kickstarted the change of our focus from SpineFrontier's fusion platform in 2014. We had to manage the AxioMed integration, dismantle the manufacturing cleanroom in Cleveland, Ohio, bring it to Boston, rebuild it, and get recertified. We also had to raise money in the millions to complete the FDA clinical IDE study and build a new team dedicated to commercializing the discs. There was just not enough time and focus left for SpineFrontier sales and R and D as we did in the past, so the revenues started to decline from 2015 steadily year after year, and our engagement with new surgeons dropped.

On the contrary, our focus on KICVentures increased, and in 2018, we made another big acquisition in NanoFuse Biologics. Similar to AxioMed, this acquisition required more investments and took focus away from SpineFrontier. We were now fully transformed to the KICventures investment holding company model. This is where we started back in 2004 with KIC and when we sold the MANTIS to Stryker Spine. We realized this is our strength and what makes us unique and that we were great at identifying disruptive technologies, developing them and engaging surgeons for feedback. With this model we set our eyes on opur first IPO and on greater focus on ambulatory surgery centers (ASC) as our target market.We began to see different market segments such as Interventional Pain Management and Neurosurgery to drive us toidentify products that we could focus on to build value as standalone portfolio companies under KICVentures Group that could seek exits. The market had returned to look for innovative, differentiated enabling technologies, just as it had in 2004 when we sold the MANTIS to Stryker. With this new market condition, we felt empowered to capitalize on our experience and wealth of technologies to build our individual portfolio companies under KICVentures, which could be tucked into the larger companies in spine surgery and pain management as mergers and acquisitions. With patience, the market had come full circle, and we needed to get ready fast. Ultimately, I envisioned us providing a suite of health technologies to enable us and other companies to improve health care delivery.

We are preparing to do so through our clinical service company, the Less Exposure Surgery Surgeon (LESS) Institute, also known as the Less Exposure Surgery (LES) Clinic, focused on providing outpatient, minimally invasive surgery care to patients and learning from each encounter. We will need to partner and hire spine surgeons and other providers.

The LESS Institute (LES Clinic) specializes in orthopedic and spine surgeries, the same areas in which KIC develops medical device solutions, giving patients better outcomes and quicker recoveries. The vast majority of surgeries we do in the LES Clinic.are done in an outpatient, ambulatory surgery center, so patients go home the same day, even when surgeries take place in the hospital. As a leader, I believe it is important to stay as close as possible to our customers to share their experiences, understand their problems, and partner with other likeminded spine surgeons. So I stay committed to treating patients and forging close relationships with surgeons even as I lead KICVentures as CEO. I think that to be a great leader, you must develop empathy and be quick to find solutions. I believe these come from understanding what people experience and being knowledgeable about all levels of your industry, so you are customer focused, and you focus on you, not on your competitors.

STAYING FOCUS AND COMMITTED TO YOUR VISION LONGTERM

Over the years, I learned it is essential to be focused and committed on my journey and learn as I go. I continue to seek new experiences, build new networks, start new companies, and develop new products to solve problems, thereby building my business expertise and leadership experience to help me achieve my success vision. Success takes time, discipline, determination, and focus. It took me ten years to consider myself a knowledgeable spine surgeon. When you are a young surgeon, you believe you are knowledgeable, but the truth is you lack the experience to realize the dangers of surgery, where you will make mistakes, so you are blindly confident with what little knowledge you gained from your training, and you want to prove that you are great. Mistakes and failures increase when you try new things, or are in new situations, or lose focus. I have made my share of mistakes to learn from on my journey to be a better surgeon. Because I wanted to learn and be better, I saw problems as opportunities to learn from and to find solutions in the form of new technologies and techniques I could patent. Issues will arise when you are forging ahead; there is no way to success without failures. If you have no failures, you are not taking on new challenges. Any new challenge results in failures first before you overcome, and you will need to innovate to succeed, which means new ways. You get stronger from failures, not from succeeding. So if you want to avoid issues or failures, which I consider critical teachable moments, you would choose to be comfortable in your situation and not change, which would be a terrible mistake, as the world will change around you, and you will be left behind.

Today, I continue to build a track record as a leader, chief executive officer, entrepreneur, investor, prolific inventor, surgeon, professor, researcher, educator, philanthropist, motivational speaker, author, spoken-word artiste, and family man. I have focused my business interest as CEO of Kingsley Investment Company (KIC) to leverage my own money to make impact investments by partnering with aligned investors, such as other surgeons, to build multiple symbiotic health care companies within the health-tech space and seek strategic partners with established companies to ultimately take one or more of our companies public in an initial public offering (IPO).

I continue to actively practice as a board-certified orthopedic and spine surgeon, treating patients in our LES Clinic outpatient setting, with the goal to deliver the best techniques and technologies to patients. I practice in Fort Lauderdale, Florida; Phoenix, Arizona; and Kingston and Montego Bay, Jamaica. I also have my medical licenses in New Jersey and New York City. I have done many surgeries in New Jersey, which felt great, considering I used to live in New Jersey before I left to Boston. We seek to build LES Clinics throughout Jamaica and the Caribbean as small, full-service, specialty outpatient hospitals, developing cutting-edge spinal instruments and devices by our own manufacturing companies under KICVentures Group and building our enterprise-based collaborative software platform to connect medical providers and patients (Mediconnects) and to help organizations connect with their members, employees, and customers remotely online (Neetworkiin). I dream of a platform on which doctors collaborate with one another and their patients and employees seamlessly. We are building the LES Society (501c3) to be an integrated society for orthopedic surgeons, neurosurgeons, pain management, physical medicine, rehabilitation doctors, and interventional radiologists to all collaborate on outpatient spine surgery treatments.

Today, many pain-management doctors and orthopedic spine surgeons have an arm's-length referral relationship, and the patient is treated based on which of the two specialists is treating them. This may often mean patients do not get the best solution available; instead, they may get the best solution according to who is deciding on the treatment. What I am describing is a process of identifying problems and converting them into business opportunities. As we deconstruct big hospitals into their individual services, I see a vision under LES Clinic to reconstruct those services back under one roof but for much smaller hospitals or outpatient ambulatory surgery centers (ASC). I follow ideas, as I believe God will give you ideas to follow and will not give it to someone else unless you don't follow it. Many people are given gifts, but they don't sow these gifts as seeds and end up with nothing or watching someone else sow the seeds and reap the harvest, which they recognize could have been theirs. They are left with hate and jealousy, hoping they fail.

As you read this book, one of the key lessons I want to convey is that I credit my success to the freedom to follow my vision to be influential and impact the world. This big vision gave me the desire to prove myself and seek others to help me prepare to succeed at a high level and to maximize my God-given abilities and opportunities. To achieve the greatest level of success, it is important that I seek to solve problems for others to benefit, invest in building a team, stay humble, remain selfless, and aggressively learn from others and any source I can find. I need to have forethought and the knowledge to anticipate and be flexible, to capitalize on opportunities that ultimately measure my growth year by year. I cannot have any fear of trying new ideas. I never judge people based on what others say. I meet them myself and form my own opinion. I want to learn every day. Those who do not want to learn will not get any help from anyone, while those who want to learn will find willing teachers, investors, and friends who will help protect them as they progress.

USE YOUR BLESSINGS TO
BUILD A LEGACY

When I realized how much I have been blessed with opportunities, I became indebted to give back to my home country of Jamaica and to my adopted country, the US, and to several people who have helped me along the way (there are too many to list here, but they know who they are, and I give my thanks). I pay special tribute to my mother, Loleta Blythe, my maternal grandmother, Birdie Dunbar, and Mr. Lloyd O. Chin, my early mentor and principal of Titchfield High School, for nurturing me and guiding me to focus on the values of education and patience. I appreciate my high school soccer coach, Donald Davis, for the discipline and drive he instilled in me to succeed at soccer and to make a loud noise so that I could be heard in Kingston and taken seriously by the media. I also thank my Jamaican Junior National coach, Bradley Stewart, who saw the potential for me to succeed as a college recruit in the US, and my Columbia University soccer coach, Dieter Ficken, and his Jamaican trainer, Norman Murray, both of whom believed in me and gave me the break I needed to get to the US.

In order to continue to prove myself, I have developed the mentality of being all in by focusing 100 percent on everything I do, big or small, giving all tasks their full dedication. I enjoy being all in with my family. Yes, I did get married again to a beautiful, intelligent, ambitious, and caring mother, Vanessa, who I met in Miami on a visit from Phoenix, Arizona, for her thirtieth birthday. I did not plan to get married again, so we lived together for many years before getting married in May 2015, after having children. I now have three children: Milan, my daughter, and Kingston and Blaze, my two sons. Milan and Kingston are my children with Vanessa. Blaze has a wonderful, dedicated, and loving mother. Having grown up without a father, I feel my most important responsibility is being a father and mentor to my children, to continue the cycle of life and ensure that the things I have learned are passed on to them as building blocks for them to achieve something even greater than I have.

My greatest legacy is leaving resources for others to utilize. I expect to do so by growing KICVentures Group to be a legacy to create jobs and opportunities for mentorship of future leaders globally. I plan to do business in every major country so entrepreneurs will have a company they can join to feel empowered and gain knowledge, support, and funding. I see this model as the way to create global leaders. I believe the way to get the greatest return from your money is by investing to build entrepreneurs and leaders with a social responsibility mantra, so the cycle continues. It would be a dream for me to aggregate my wealth with others to build this philanthropic investment paradigm under KIC and build a leadership institute under Prove Yourself Institute.. Speaking as a Black man, growing KIC also means building a private equity platform that can invest in the next generation of Black leadership.

It is my Wakanda strategy to build wealth in a predominantly Black country, such as in Jamaica, and investments in the US and then invest in other predominantly Black countries and Africa. I believe with a deep conviction that helping budding entrepreneurs is the greatest generational legacy of philanthropy and a smart way to generate a great return on investment with the broadest impact. There is a lot in this section of the book, and it may seem exhausting to follow. This would be a true reflection of how it felt for me living my life on the fast track, moving like a shark, never resting. Therefore, I thank you for sharing this book and hope there is something special in it to help you achieve the greatest successes on your journey to prove yourself. Remember: be eager to learn, be humble, invest in others, plant your gifts as seeds, and never quit as you endeavor to succeed in life and business at the same time.

INTRODUCTION

Let's get into this book. If you want to succeed, where do you start? Are you going hard enough? Having trouble in your pursuit? Do you think success is about luck? Or can you learn how to succeed? At the end of the day, you can ask yourself all the questions and have all the doubt, but regardless of the answers, you must recognize the time to start. And for those pursuing success in its truest form, that time is now.

Let's start with a personal question: do you feel the desire to succeed or to prove yourself? If you ever felt the need to prove yourself, you have that essential first spark for success—called desire.

As I embarked on writing this book, I thought of how I first felt the need to succeed in life and to prove myself early in my childhood. For me, it began in Buff Bay, a tiny seaside town in Portland, Jamaica, where I was born to a single teenage mother. I reflected on how this strong desire drove me to make it all the way to the best Ivy League schools in the US, to work on Wall Street, to graduate with a medical degree with honors from Harvard Medical School, to become a board-certified orthopedic spine surgeon, to be the chief executive officer of KICVentures Group Inc., with a net worth of over a billion dollars and growing, and to make time to have a family with three children. The question is, if I did all this, are there lessons and principles you can learn from my journey? Read on to learn how you can also develop the principles of success to improve your life's journey, to start your own business, or to rise through the ranks of any organization or corporation.

This book describes real business experiences and recounts private anecdotes from my journey to illustrate lessons that led to my success in life. Written in twelve powerful chapters, it promises to help you on your journey to succeed in life and business. As you read, you will likely see similarities in your life. When you do, share your own lessons, and join our movement to empower new entrepreneurs to build multimillion-dollar businesses.. Prove to yourself and others that you will succeed, and when you do, you will enjoy the respect and lifestyle of successful people.

If you have never felt the need to prove yourself, you will have that feeling by the end of this book. When you feel like proving you can accomplish something, whether it is to prove to yourself or to others, you will experience an inner force awakening inside that will urge you to succeed and make an impact in this life. Society needs people like you to start businesses and to discover new and better ways to do things to keep the engine of our civilization going. Success is not free, so you must learn how to earn it. You have to learn how to be all in, to give 100 percent effort and focus. What if we all decided not to seek success and not to create new businesses? Our society, more than ever, embraces and rewards innovation and sees the value in chasing success. You have the potential within yourself to start and build a successful business or to rise through the ranks and become a well-respected leader.

You don't control the situation into which you were born, and if you are not in a great position with a lot of resources right now, believe in yourself and believe that you can control where you end up or where you are heading. Like many people who desired success and achieved it, I grew up poor. I was not privy to many resources or financial wealth. When I realized my true situation, I became hungry and developed a desire for success, financial security, and independence, but I had to come up with a plan and start the journey to learn how to succeed.

To start a journey, you need a path. My path began with observing and listening to anyone around me who seemed to have success, and then using my drive and resourcefulness, I began my own success journey. Along the way, I set small, reachable goals, laying the foundation of getting an education, being inquisitive to learn from others, honing my athletic abilities, and sharpening my competitiveness. Essentially, I began early in life to prepare to be successful, and you will also need to go through a process of preparation in your own life.

Because of this preparation, when the opportunity knocked on my door to go to Columbia University on a soccer scholarship, I was ready to answer the call. And when I landed in New York, I arrived in a place where I felt resources were at my fingertips; I could prove to myself that I was capable of achieving my greatest desires in life. I could finally prove to all those who helped me (my mother, my siblings and other relatives, my friends, my community, and my country, all those who paved the way for me to have opportunities they did not have) that I could rise to the highest levels in life and business. When you start at the bottom, you learn how to be resourceful, to succeed with what you have and not wait for more resources you believe you need or want. Through trial and error, active planning, and being willing to learn quickly and make changes without fear, I discovered how to be resourceful and set goals to succeed over and over again. My question to you is this: since I have done it, why shouldn't you learn from my lessons? If you are already on the path to success, then this book should reinforce many of the fundamental lessons you have already learned, and you can enjoy reflecting on your own experiences as you share mine.

In a nutshell, as you read this book, be ready to learn lessons that will prepare you to reach high levels of success at a faster pace, because time is limited. As you read each chapter, take notes and create visions of how you could apply these lessons and refresh yourself over and over. Be smart, be sensible, learn principles from others, and use them to succeed. Avoid being stubborn or arrogant and thinking you already have all the answers. Too often, if we are arrogant, we are also stubborn, so we keep repeating the same mistakes, although circumstances may change, not even realizing it, hoping to succeed each time, thinking we are trying something different or that with just more time and money, we will succeed.

Or we may choose to stay in our situation, afraid to lose what we have and not seeing that we really have no control. Life is passing us by as we work our fingers to the bone to maintain our current lifestyles, trading time for money or sheltering beneath our titles. We find ourselves so deep in our situation we are afraid that if we try to look somewhere else, we will lose what we have. I often hear people say it is their character to be conservative or frugal, so they will not invest to multiply what money they already have stored, for fear of losing. Or we feel we just don't have the time to spare or the resources to succeed beyond our current situation. Many times, what is being said is "Until I am forced to change my situation, I will not change, nor will I take any risk." The greatest risk, they don't realize, is not changing and not investing some of the money they work so hard to obtain. Whatever you do, you will end up dead at the end of it all. Living is a gift, so take risks to get the most out of life before it ends.

If trying to avoid risks sounds familiar, be mindful of this scenario, because in the end, you could be missing key opportunities and trading health and time for wealth, while being sucked into a vicious time vortex where you are focused on transactional activities to make money that you then spend to get by, rather than investing time and money into improving your life. If you are not changing, seeking new opportunities, and creating partnerships that save you time and give you financial independence, you are standing still by working to maintain what you have or going backward, because the world is moving by you when you are trying to maintain things the same as they are and missing opportunities. Reading a book like this is proactive; you are preparing for when opportunities come, and you will learn that even if you are on the right path for success, you will be in a better position if you find ways to collaborate with other successful people. The more successful friends you make, the more likely you will get out of trouble or save yourself if you are heading into bankruptcy. In sharing my story, there is nothing in it to suggest that I was destined for a successful life. Nor was I simply lucky. If anything, I was always searching for new opportunities and new relationships, reading, studying, observing, preparing along the way so that when opportunities appeared, I was trained and ready to capitalize.

This book will help you on your journey if you learn from my experiences, struggles, and victories. I hope it will inspire you to believe that you, too, can feel empowered to live your life in pursuit of success and financial independence. By believing this, you will realize you can achieve your greatest potential. And the rewards of a successful lifestyle are worth every sacrifice along your journey. You will be energized to act on your desire to succeed. You will appreciate that your greatest resources are your time and health; you must treasure both, not wasting them. You will learn about the value of money and that success is an individual journey, but you don't have to feel alone at the top when you succeed, because you will have the tools to surround yourself with a core management team to buy into your vision and build alongside you as they feel a sense of ownership and growth.

From sharing in my experiences, you will look at your life and see that every person who turned their back on you or closed a door in your face will motivate you to focus your efforts elsewhere, surround yourself with the right people, and seek the right doors. Be a light wherever you go in your zest for life, your thirst for learning, and your desire to be influential and impact the world. As you rise, you will be the nail that sticks up, and they will want to hammer you over the head for you to conform and fit into their design. Success in your own way will be your vindication, and you will get great satisfaction from knowing you chose to be different, to follow your vision and prove yourself. But after you achieve success, remember to put people first and share your successes, to make lives better for those who helped you and those you can help. Fall in love with seeking to help winners win or partners with winners to help you win. Network to build relationships that you can provide value to, and in return, they can provide you value. This is how you will protect yourself against failures. However, keep your close circle small. Avoid losers, people who only care about themselves and their success, as they will befriend you and eventually cut you deep when you need them the most. Get ready. Let's read each of the following essential keys and be inspired to go live a successful life and build a successful business to create a legacy that helps society be a better place.

CHAPTER 1
ESSENTIAL KEY #1
START WITH A DESIRE TO SUCCEED
AND SATISFY A NEED

Getting a desire is like starting a fire. Maybe you are just thinking of starting a fire, or you have the wood piled up to start the fire, or maybe you have just a few embers that are just starting to ignite. There are other stages of starting a fire, but maybe you fall within one of the stages I described. When I think of my fire, it seemed I was thinking of starting a fire as a young boy, and once I got to high school, I began to pile up the woods to set them ablaze. As the years went by, I kept seeking mentors, new knowledge, and experiences, which was like adding wood and fuel to the fire, and it just got taller and wider, and so did my desires. Over time, I have kept the fire more controlled and protected, so it is always burning, and at times it blazes, then goes back down to a controlled burn. There are even times when it seems the fire is going to be extinguished. Regardless of how my fire is burning on the outside, what helps me is how, on the inside, I always feel like I am blazing to be a force of nature, fierce in my desire to succeed. I feel like I am at war within myself. This might be my Zodiac sign speaking, as I am an Aries god of war. I am my worst critic, and at the same time, I am my biggest cheerleader and motivator. With all this sense of being at war on the inside, it leads to me constantly feeling a strong desire to achieve, so I am changing and moving, not stopping, like a hungry shark. I believe this constant movement attracts and finds opportunities in the form of problems to be solved and needs to be satisfied.

It is essential to build a desire to satisfy a need if you want to succeed. The need could be your need or the need as an opportunity for you to solve a problem, to create a customer and a business to serve that customer and others to follow. Follow a need to be of service to others who look to you for a solution. Philippians 2:3 says do nothing out of selfish ambition or vain conceit. Rather, in humility, value others above yourself. Maybe it is a philanthropic need or a humanitarian need. Find some need that is going to feed back to light your desire fire or set it ablaze and create customers who will benefit. My burning desire attracts the people who want to be part of a vision to make an impact. Together we can build the working team to execute the vision. To the world, I am a go-getter, which is the result of the inner fire from my desire to achieve my vision. All of this bottled-up fire is what fuels my desire and energizes me to want to get up every day and live life to the fullest.

So how do you get your desire? Let's get into this first chapter about the first essential, desire. I will spend the most time on this topic of all the lessons, as I believe you should spend the most time at the beginning of any journey, planning and learning before you go.

I did not wake up one day and suddenly have the desire to start a business or become a CEO. Few entrepreneurs I know did this. It all started long before from the desire to succeed, to satisfy my need for financial freedom, security, and the lifestyle that comes with it and to be influential and make an impact in this world. To impact the world, I started with the question, what needs or problems can I solve? First, there were my needs, to improve myself to prepare myself to achieve. Self-improvement results from investing in activities that make you better than you were the day before. Many people don't improve and therefore do not have the desire to achieve anything. They try to maintain their current self, which means trying to be comfortable. Most people desire to progress but procrastinate and never start or finish the journey, so they never progress in life or business. As I became more equipped, solving health care problems became the desire that touched my soul. I feel this is my calling and the biggest driver of my desire, baked by focus on my big vision. See how my vision feeds my desire?

When that desire builds up enough, you will know it is time to take that first step to visualize a path, and when you see a path, that is the moment to embark on your journey to achieve a personal goal, like starting your own business or getting more formal education, or seeking mentorship—three decisions that I believe are important to your success. A journey starts with that first step on a path, whether it is a path that is already there, a path you are already on, or one that you will beat down the bushes to create. The first step is easy, but it's hard to make the decision, while the last few steps to success are very hard work, but by then, you are usually strong and determined.

Those who have talent and the means to be great at whatever they do may go through life always doing great at every level, from high school and college to graduate school and their ultimate job, and then to a house in the suburbs with the white picket fence, behind which they are a great parent, with 2.5 children, according to the statistics for middle-class success. This is a real achievement by the way, and for many of us, this is a wonderfully successful life. If you fit this profile, it is probable that you are always told you do great at whatever you put your mind to. You feel you are already doing well, so you live a comfortable life enjoying the niceties of life that money can buy. You are comfortable in every way, so why change? Well, congratulations on a great start to a successful life. You may discover during this book that you have the potential for greater successes. If you are comfortable today, it is likely you don't feel the need to change what you are doing or to invest in learning any different information from what you already know is working to sustain your current lifestyle. If it is not broken, why fix it? I want you to read this book and develop a desire for impact instead of a comfort with just doing great in your current situation. Comfort from a comfortable life is a ticking time bomb, but comfort from an uncomfortable life means you will always be comfortable, no matter the life situation. It also means you will be changing and not waiting for crises to change your life (then you find yourself reacting). It means you will face crises and uncomfortable situations to overcome to get to the next level above your crises.

Once you set your vision, it is like putting down roots. The roots of a tree stay firm as long as the tree is alive and growing. However, different branches form with leaves and even fruits, so you will try different things, like branches, and different goals, like fruits. I make sure that I form branches that are connected to the same tree, and the fruits I bear go back into fertilizing the root of the tree and bring value. Too many people try to plant too many trees in their life, so they move from one tree to the next new tree, usually in the form of new jobs. The most successful people will plant a tree that they own and will nurture it to create the greatest harvest with time that is recurring. If they plant other trees, it is to create alternative revenue pipelines and an even bigger harvest. What I am describing here is what KICVentures Group has done. We have many companies in our portfolio generating revenues, while others are creating value so we can have multiple revenue pipelines to harvest.

As you learn to develop your desire, aim to build upon your vision, and if you find yourself forming desires that are offshoots of your main vision, ensure the offshoots are branches first. If they are new trees, make sure you can nurture them. I like to look at a strong, tall tree that rises above the many trees making up the forest. This is how I see big, successful companies and their founders; they rise to great heights with their success above the field.

Bill Gates, the founder of Microsoft and one of the richest people in the world, stands like a tall tree in the forest of entrepreneurs. He chose an uncomfortable path and focused on growing himself when he left Harvard after two years; so did Mark Zuckerberg, founder of Facebook. Steve Jobs, founder of Apple, did not graduate from college either. These tree legends had such a strong desire to pursue the opportunities they saw that not even not completing college distracted them from following their desires. See the power of desire? I would imagine all their fellow classmates were comfortably on their way to graduate in a few years and eager to go to graduate school next. These three pioneers chose the discomfort of entrepreneurship, followed their desires urgently, paved new paths, and were rewarded with great financial success, impact, and legacy.

I finished my time at Columbia University and graduate school at Harvard Medical School. Most people who succeed graduate from college and even get advanced formal education. I did not have an urgent opportunity to build the desire to pursue that would prompt me to drop out of college. I also believed completing college was an important success goal to build upon. In my case, I was the first in my family to go to college, so completing college was a major milestone, not one in which I had a compelling substitute. However, I was hungry enough to make any decision, even to leave before I finished my degrees if I had a clear vision that required me to be full-time 100 percent, but I did not have it, so I stayed and graduated each time. At Harvard, I joined a research laboratory under my mentor, Dr. Michael Rosenblatt, and founded a number of companies as I explored entrepreneurship while attending classes. I avoided being comfortable in a bubble, like most students pursuing a degree. I find that when you are enrolled in a program, you follow the program someone sets for you and mandates for you to follow. When you are in the real world, you have to parent yourself to come up with the program and make decisions. In the real world, you need strong desire to discipline yourself and drive you to take decisive actions. You need resilience and perseverance to see your decisions come to pass.

The Wright brothers, Orville and Wilbur, from Dayton, Ohio, labored for years to realize their desire to fly an airplane. Their first successful flight occurred December 17, 1903, for just twelve seconds, 120 feet (37 meters) in Kitty Hawk, North Carolina. Today, their pioneering work has impacted the world immeasurably. Every day, the world is connected by airplanes, with people flying over thousands of miles. The point here is that we need to open our eyes to look for an opportunity that will spark our desire to pursue, no matter how small, because the desire is the first spark for any journey, and the end result may impact the world and move us all forward. This is a journey to a life of purpose and fulfillment. So many people find this desire in the form of a company that is rising, but they get sidetracked by the lure of a new job that pays them more after they have gotten experience. They trade an experience to succeed with a company for something with more immediate tangible rewards. When you stick with the pursuit of success, you will go through lots of trials, but use these moments to strengthen your desire. Stick with it and grow your resilience so you can succeed in a big way and then be equipped to go start your own company or become a leader within the company.

I had no idea what the journey would be like when, as a young boy in poor, rural Jamaica, I told my mother that I wanted to go to the United States or to England by any means necessary. I also told her I would not go to the airport in Kingston to see people off unless it was I who was traveling on the plane overseas to make my life better. Back then, I developed that desire, and I set it as a goal and decided I would succeed by studying hard and getting an academic scholarship, or by practicing hard and getting an athletic scholarship. Maybe get both. I was so driven. I remember studying late at night in my grandmother's one-bedroom home, with the dining table against the wall and the two beds next to the table. She only had a kerosene lamp for light, so I had to be studying close to the lamp to see. One night, I could see her twisting and turning, finding it hard to sleep. She then blurted out in frustration as to what could I be studying so much to be up this late with the lamp on? I was too driven to learn and succeed. I kept focused on studying night after night, and eventually she got used to my consistency and commitment. She eventually became proud of my discipline with time.

Another example of my strong desire to succeed happened when I started to play soccer officially on a team when I was around eleven years old. Before that, I played soccer barefooted. It rained a lot in Buff Bay, since we were on the windward side of the Blue Mountains. The field could be soaked with water, and the ball and grass were slippery. If we played against a visiting team when it rained, we expected to win. Now that I was on a team, it was required for me to wear a shoe of some kind to play in games. I couldn't afford to buy soccer shoes. Neither could my mother, nor would she if she could, since she was all about education, not sports. I saved and eventually bought a pair of Chinese ballet footwear, made of black cloth and a brown rubber sole. They were very flexible, so it was close to still being barefooted. However, when the field was wet, it was difficult to make moves, so I had to adjust my moves to short bursts and shoot the ball after I made a move. My uncle Winston "Sheriff" Chin was always supportive of me, so he helped me reach out to my uncle Everald in London, England, who sent me a watch and a pair of soccer cleats by the brand name Stylo. I got the watch stolen after I hid it behind the goal post one day when I was playing a game at my high school field. I have always loved watches since and fostered the desire to one day build a collection of fine watches. The Stylo cleats were hard for me since they had long studs designed for English soccer conditions. The adjustment was tough, going from bare feet to Chinese ballet footwear to soccer cleats. During this time, I was feeding my desire to succeed at soccer and was willing to devote myself to succeed any way I could. I needed to get an academic or athletic scholarship to the USA, and the clock was ticking, so I had to go hard every day.

Fast-forward to years later, and I realize that ever since I was a boy, I have been patient whenever I follow my desire to succeed, and with time, the universe provides me with great rewards. My desire to succeed meant I would boldly go along new paths and start new journeys with new goals, with the faith that success would come with time and hard work. I had also developed the habit to pursue multiple paths to the same goal to amplify my chances for success and diversify my risks for failure. These habits have become traits that I continue today as a leader.

I did stick to my words and went to the Kingston airport in 1984. This time, I was flying to New York to enroll at Columbia University's Columbia College as a top soccer recruit in the United States of America. I was given the opportunity to achieve great academic goals at a prestigious Ivy League college, so I was determined to make the most of the opportunity. As a result, I dedicated myself to helping the team win games. At the end of my senior year, I achieved the honor of Ivy League Player of the Year in soccer. I also had the desire to develop into a leader, so I ran for student government and was unanimously voted by my peers to be the president of the student government for the senior class. I became the first Black student to achieve this position, and unfortunately, I think it still stands that I am the only Black student in over 374 years of the Ivy League to be president of a senior class. I was energized graduating from Columbia University and ready to conquer the next level to fuel my desire to achieve my big vision.

The desire to succeed will push you to be strategic and patient. After college, I decided I needed to get a job before graduate school so I could have some business experience. I chose to work in a consulting firm so I could get different experiences. I worked as a management information systems consultant at Andersen Consulting (now Accenture) in Manhattan. I also set a new desire to go to Wall Street, which came through, and I spent six months there. Coming off the subway and walking up the stairs to Wall Street, seeing the mass of business people in suits, and then entering Goldman Sachs to sit at my desk left me feeling I was insignificant and not on the right path to my vision. By now, I had developed trust in myself and my instincts as to what desires and paths to follow. I decided I needed to get into health care investments but first to become a doctor so that I could work for myself to build a practice where my patients were my customers and my success depended upon me. I also thought I could marry business and medicine to be an investment banker, for example focused on health care investments. So I left New York City in 1992 and went to Boston to study medicine at the best medical school in the world, Harvard Medical School. This opportunity again fueled my desire to excel, and I graduated with a medical degree with honors.

I was building consistency in excellence; I try to make all my activities about the desire for excellence, for greatness, and setting goals to achieve my desires, no matter how small. This is the way to progress: have the desire to achieve something, set initiatives and goals, and close on them as soon as possible. Small goals are a great way to build the habit of succeeding, and as time goes on, you will achieve larger goals and be more efficient with your time to take on more and more goals.

This approach can become a habit for you, as it is for me. Habits become you when you do them over and over, so practice good habits. It is satisfying for me when people describe me by my traits, and on the inside, I know that these are habits that I work hard to be consistent at, doing well and automatically, not given to me by birth. You can read this book and believe me, or you can find your own way. It won't change the fact that goal setting is a habit of success, and the desire to succeed is essential to finding a path and starting your journey. For me, it started with a vision, and this vision is like the lighthouse that I keep referring to, to keep on track, and the darker the nights, the brighter my vision shines to light the path for me to keep going. Small successes are the best way I know of to build your desires and confidence over time and to keep you disciplined. Small goals are like scoring from close to the goal, while big goals are like winning the match. Start with setting reachable goals and count your scores, no matter how small. We have all heard that we should count our blessings. Do that, and count your successes too.

In 2005, when I founded KIC, and years later our venture subsidiary, KICVentures Group, to invest and build health technology companies, I did not know the extent to which I was embarking on a journey that would grow into a portfolio of health-tech and information technology (IT) companies, valued at over a billion dollars in ten years. I get asked about our valuation from people who doubt that I could have a billion-dollar company. This is common when you do not have third-party validation, such as by the media. You will be tested to prove your personal value and the valuation of your company. Jeff Bezos was seeking $25,000– $50,000 from individual investors when he valued Amazon at $6 million. Even then, investors forced him to drop his valuation down to $5 million. The point is to know your value and your company value and communicate that value as an expert and authority. This means you must be a salesperson. I think the best way to be an effective salesperson is to have a genuine desire to succeed at convincing someone that you have something valuable that will satisfy their need. Your desire will be reflected in your knowledge and enthusiasm, which make you likable and respected. This means you must know what you are selling and to whom you are selling, so much so that you are seen as an authority on what you are selling. You then have the control of the sales cycle, which needs to be as fast as possible, as the longer you take to sell someone, the less likely it is they will buy.

So it did not matter that I did not know how long it would take to succeed or if the journey was going to be hard. I knew my true situation before I decided to start building companies. I knew that I did not fit any stereotype for a successful entrepreneur, being Black and coming from a small town in Jamaica. I did not have a track record of investment success, working for a large investment company with connections to financial institutions that would be a source of funding for my companies as an entrepreneur. At the time, I did not graduate from a prestigious business school and fit into the network. I did not have a lot of personal cash to finance any business to a high level. I did not seek out opportunities to be mentored by a successful entrepreneur in person since I did not have access or the qualifications to interest a business mentor. I had no family connections to fall back on, nor was I born with money. These are wonderful scenarios to have access to, but I did not have any of them to fall back on. I was going to have to start from the bottom, using my own two hands and my own intellect to prove myself and be self-reliant. This is typical of an entrepreneur and more so of a Black solopreneur like me, striking out with a big vision and no re-sources. If this is you, this is where you start: look at your situation, get ready, get set, and then go. It is essential that you recognize your true situation before you embark on your journey. Be determined in your desire to learn fast and deeply about the subject of interest and the industry so you build confidence and enthusiasm, both of which create passion. Passion and desire are like brothers or sisters; they are closely related.

To be self-reliant, I knew we needed our own source of cash to grow our businesses. You have to develop a hustle mentality to consider any option to get cash in your hands, because with cash, dreams are possible and can become reality; without it, they become impossible, and you wake up. That's why I started to develop my ideas into patents in 2000. I was hoping to sell one, but nobody was buying patents. It's why in 2004 I started to develop one of the patents into a percutaneous pedicle screw product for minimally invasive surgery of the lumbar spine. I called this product the Minimal Access Nontraumatic Insertion System (MANTIS); this became my first medical device company under KIC. I developed two patents for this MANTIS system and sold them and the assets of the company to Stryker, a publicly traded company, in 2005. Now I had cash and experience to start thinking bigger and bolder.

I could have taken the ideas further along and created greater value for a larger future payout, but I needed cash to fuel my big vision, so I made a deal that gave me immediate cash over future cash. I admit this was a terrible agreement since I should have kept royalties and earned future cash. You will learn that agreements are very important to your success or failure, so seek the right advisers and try to make sure your agreements are given lots of considerations for the present and future. Mistakes like this will happen for you to learn lessons. It is part of the journey. I have had to learn to let it go and use the experience to drive my desire to prove I can succeed again.

With the cash from the MANTIS sale, I started on my way to build KIC's portfolio and eventually consolidate under KICVentures Group as our health care investment holding company, to fund all portfolio companies through mergers, acquisitions, or start-ups. The money we made from any of the portfolio companies was reinvested to build our cash and portfolio organically, and over time, we would likely get another big sale. I called this our blockbuster strategy. This means that we use what money we have to build a portfolio we can afford, aiming for one of the portfolio companies to hit it huge and launch KICVentures Group big-time toward being listed on the public market in the USA. We are still building toward this goal, but like I said before, focus on your small successes and avoid focusing on spectacular goals that can become spectacular failures before you are ready. It's like climbing a ladder; focus on one rung at a time after you set the ladder against the right wall. Small goals help you stay alive and keep building, making progress, and preparing you to fight future battles. Remember to get your life SET: to *survive* and *evolve* before you *thrive.*

There were still many naysayers and haters along the way who dismissed me. Some did not tell me to my face that I was not going to succeed. It was what they did not say, how they said what they said, or the way they avoided helping me or investing alongside me, even when they knew that they stood to benefit by working with me to pool our resources. Many successful surgeons were content with the money they made doing surgeries; I also made lots of money as a surgeon but invested it all into the businesses to build more money. Others felt I should stay inside the surgeon box and excluded me from their institutions, as I seemed too different, too risky.

You see, it was never my desire to own a grape or be a consumer of other people's grapes. I wanted to own a vineyard and build an organization to grow grapes and make wine or whatever we chose; I knew it would take a lot of work, and we would at some point need investors and customers. But getting others interested in helping you is difficult because everyone wants to own grapes but not a vineyard. Worse, they don't believe you can succeed at building a vineyard since you are no smarter than they are, and they don't see themselves growing a vineyard when they can get grapes easily. Don't hate back; those are not your people. Find a way to get the right people to invest as partners or be your customers. To build a vineyard takes time, humility, and an unstoppable desire to succeed. When you succeed, remember it is human nature to doubt in one moment and in the next moment to jump on the success bandwagon and celebrate your success.

I want to return to the grape metaphor for a moment. It does not matter that you have the knowledge to grow the vineyard and the drive to take care of it; people with money or the ability to help you in other ways will not have the vision to see that, together, you could grow a vineyard. The people you employ might not have the commitment necessary to stay the course on the journey to success. They may have trouble seeing the vineyard happening and how they will benefit. Many times, you as an entrepreneur will not be understood. You are too different.

The hardest pill to swallow will come from the ones you thought would support your businesses by investing, being customers, or some other way within their means. They will make it clear in what they say or how they avoid you that you will not get their support; they may even support your competition. They will remind you that you have skin in the game, and they don't. They will ignore the obvious fact that this is exactly what you are asking them to do: to put their skin in the game. Some may still talk with you as if everything is all cool, as long as it does not involve your business, while others will stop returning your calls because they expect it will be a call about your business. The people you help on their journey will forget about you once they feel they don't need you anymore. Others will be so caught up in themselves and their success and titles that they will be too busy surviving to see any benefits in working with you. Others just want to be close enough to watch you, hoping to witness you failing; your failure feels like their success. There are the ones with large egos who will copy you but make it look as if they are just as successful as you as they partner with your competition. I imagined how successful many National Basketball Association (NBA) players would be had they partnered with Michael Jordan in his brand deal with Nike. Today, Jordan is a billionaire from his Nike brand deal, and many of the players in the NBA retire with no deals to sustain them financially. They do not have their own brand from pursuing their own deal versus partnering with Jordan on his Nike deal. I don't know if this would be successful, but Jordan would be foolish to turn down a great deal that would expand his brand image and sell more products.

DESIRE VERSUS THE BLACK
ENTREPRENEUR DILEMMA

Being a successful Black entrepreneur in the USA is rare. As a Black person in America, you are likely the first or second person, or you are among the first or second generation in your family to go to college. So just graduating and getting a job or having a professional degree like a doctor, engineer, or lawyer is major success. Chances are many of your friends and colleagues are not super wealthy and successful either, so you are not around lots of people who are role models for you to follow or to network with, to pull you up to a higher level or invest in your ideas for a start-up business as an entrepreneur. I found that this leaves Black entrepreneurs feeling alone, vulnerable, and afraid. Their desire to succeed is not the problem; it is their desire to keep going against all odds as Black entrepreneurs, knowing there is no support available. The obstacles and traps are always trying to kill our progress. The hardest feeling to face is the feeling that Black people will not support you either and may be quick to sabotage you to keep you from rising above them. Successful Black professionals enjoy being the *first* or *only*, so you threaten that title as you rise. If, like me, you are the only one, then it signals that you already took the title—hence the jealousy and sabotage. This is the crab in a barrel mentality. Not everyone has this mentality, but it feels like everyone when you cannot find any support from your own people. When I think about how Black people struggle as individuals and how much smarter it would be if we were to pool our resources, it is frustrating. The second feeling is that people would rather you not try, since they fear that you will fail, and they will somehow feel like failures by association.

As Black people, we love the symbolism of one of our own suc-ceeding. It makes us feel proud. It is the same on the flip side; when one of us tries to do something different and we fail, it makes us feel let down. Many times, we see a successful Black entrepreneur who makes it, but we don't agree with the way they live their lives or who they marry or associate with outside the Black race. It does not matter to us that we were not there supporting them when they were trying to succeed. As a Black entrepreneur, the odds are overwhelmingly high that you will not have access to funding, so you have to survive with the feeling of being on the verge of running out of money. Crazy to think that over 98 percent of the trillions in funding in America goes to White males, yet we as Black males don't realize that we must look out for ourselves.

As a Black entrepreneur, your desire to continue will be tested daily. This can be a great motivator if it does not break you, so keep trying. Never quit, despite the odds against you. Maybe you are more optimistic about Black people supporting you, so you decide you will seek support to get investments or to use your product or partner with you as a fellow Black person. I would applaud your optimism and say go ahead, but first depend on yourself. I could write a book on just this section from my efforts and the realization that I needed to depend on me, not on anybody else, regardless of race. I learned to make business friends who see the value in investing in my companies. My opinions about what I experienced as a lack of support from Black people are not restricted to the Black experience. I believe it applies to any group that you as an entrepreneur find yourself being associated with, since people in your group will not easily be your cheerleader when you are starting out and not yet successful. This often applies to family members not supporting you in the way you would hope. Why? I think groupthink leads to the sense that everyone is equal and just as capable, and they will have difficulty seeing your rise over theirs. I see this in my profession as a spine surgeon. Despite being the only Black spine surgeon to own companies that develop medical devices for spine surgery—and we believe we have superior devices and instruments—there is no sense among spine surgeons that I am doing anything special, with value worth partnering with me. So they focus on their own survival and

seek to work with brand-name, established medical device companies who play to the surgeons' egos while collecting millions in
revenues from their sweat.

So what do you do as an entrepreneur? Accept that you will have
to seek the right partners to network with, who will appreciate the
opportunity to work with you and who can see how the story is a
fit for them. You will not be celebrated on your way up, only when
you succeed. Be assured that when you succeed, it immediately becomes easier to attract supporters who were not there for you when
you were trying to succeed. I have learned to promote my successes.
Without promotion, it will seem that you are doing nothing. You
will face obstacles of all forms, and these will always be there as you
grow. Despite obstacles, creating new customers and innovating are
the purposes of your business, and if you do so and your product is
innovative, then investors will happen with time, but you will need
to have the desire, right story, and perseverance.

Let me be real. If you are a Black entrepreneur, you will realize
you have to be the best and work the hardest and smartest and still
feel you are at a disadvantage in getting support because you are
Black, but you must use that as motivation to seek new paths. You
will need relationships and capital to get ahead, but you have to
battle being Black and unusual to get their attention, and you have a
high bar to overcome to be trusted as qualified. The more I succeed,
the more I sense the vibes that there was jealousy, and this translated
into action that said loudly, "Why should I help him succeed and
rise above me? Why should I even give him recognition? He won't
make it anyway, so I should distance myself." All people gravitate
to hype, so promote yourself and your success to people who are
able to see your success without feeling threatened. If other people
are promoting your story, then people will see you as a success, but
not the people who see you as a friend or part of their group above
their own sense of success. This will change once you get that one
big success. Then they will change toward you and recognize you

for succeeding. It's like the Olympics of life. Once you succeed on camera in front of the world, people who know you will celebrate you from afar, as they feel part of your success, despite never supporting you before. I think we have so few successes in the Black business communities that when we do see success, we partake regardless of color. So brand recognition is big with us, and we use brands as status symbols to associate ourselves with success so that we, in return, seem successful. In the medical device industry, it means surgeons gravitate to the big companies as a status symbol to portray that they are successful because they can name-drop the big company. For an upstart Black entrepreneur without a brand name, it is difficult to get Black support. We just do not have a history of collective support with community benefits and legacy wealth creation to make us circulate our money within Black businesses. In theory, we understand how it would be smart, but in practice, it takes too much effort. We don't have a platform on which we can honestly discuss the issue of supporting Black businesses proactively. We don't have a Black Wall Street anymore as a center of excellence that could demonstrate success that others can follow. We are probably unique in that any racial or ethnic group can come into a Black neighborhood and open a store and outperform the local Black store. So, too, in the medical device industry, where Black surgeons fit in with the White status medical device companies and do not have any desire to partner with a Black-owned medical device company. Black businesses face this dilemma even when we can prove apples to apples we have superior products and would form a more supportive customer experience. There is just no real movement to emotionally attract us to Black businesses, nor is there enough presence to be a daily reminder.

There is an old saying: the Black man's ice is not as cold as the White man's ice. Even when you do get in front of Black customers or investors, they are suspicious of you, as it is not their natural expectation to support a Black business, although it is politically correct to say they support all Black businesses. In health care, it is even more unexpected to get Black support since there is no history of Black people investing and building wealth in health care technologies, at least not to my knowledge. I would not be such an enigma if there were successful Black medical device entrepreneurs that I could follow who made billions. This fact is a motivator for me, as I feel a sense of legacy to be the one to raise the flag up a flagpole so another Black entrepreneur can look up for inspiration on their own climb. Having someone to keep you grounded on your journey means you are less likely to be fearful, since there is a path already laid down. Instead, you might just need to create a branch. There is less of a natural inclination for Black people with money to seek investment opportunities in health care companies versus more tangible day-to-day consumer products and software applications they feel they have a better understanding of. Real estate is attractive to Black surgeons. It seems like a no-lose investment since they believe they understand real estate and that real estate always goes up in value.

Some of us love the symbolism of a Black person we don't know personally succeeding; it gives us a sense of value, but we were absent when that person was struggling, trying to make it. This might explain why many financially successful Black people don't support helping other Black people succeed. This leads to a cycle of individual Black successes that are far and few between. Another of my observations is the mentality that there are only so many of us who will succeed, so if one of us succeeds, it usually means we are the first or only one, and this designation feels great. But what happens when someone else is in that position? We think there will not be another, so let's just hate on that person since it is not us. It is easier emotionally for us to sabotage versus support when we see someone similar to us succeeding above us. This is human nature and part of groupthink. Seeing a successful Black person coming out of similar situations who has risen above us may energize us to compete to be recognized. Instead of collaborating, I see us going to fit in with a competitor so we can get status there and be the first or only Black person. A successful Black person who has crossover appeal is usually celebrated by everyone, but there will be a fair share of haters who will label them as not being Black enough anymore—therefore a sellout. My observations may be painful to read, but as I mentioned above, these are my opinions from observations and not from any research, and I believe there is enough truth to spark self-assessment. I believe Black economic and political empowerment is necessary if we are to achieve broad success as a race, so I would rather put my thoughts out there than be silent. If you are not Black, you might find that these observations apply to your experience among your friends. Develop the desire and perseverance to find alternative ways to succeed, where your race is not a handicap. In other words, use race as a motivator to build your desire to succeed and prove yourself. Then tell your story.

What about White racism? As a Black entrepreneur, I experience White racism as more of a systemic social problem. For example, it's very difficult to get private equity investment as a Black entrepreneur. We are just not the targets, nor do we have the access. Women suffer similar problems, so it is not just a race problem. It is just the way the system is set up by White men in powerful companies for White men. The majority of the money for funding is controlled by these White men who thrive in the financial institutions, where they inherit the privileges and the knowledge. There is no conspiracy; it is just the legacy. They tend to follow their formulas and stay within their networks and comfort areas. People with money are not racist because they have money. Money attracts money, and Black people on a large scale do not have money to play in the money circle. I don't experience White racism at the individual person level, only at the institutional level. When I approach someone who has money, it begins and ends with the opportunity and whether I am someone in whom people with their hard-earned money want to invest. Being White does not get you investors. You need to play the game to win investors. This is why you read a book like this, to develop yourself to become a compelling success story and attract success, which happens when you exude a burning desire to succeed.

I get most of my support from White investors and customers. I believe this is based on the measure of whether I have something of value or not. For example, I have had White spine surgeons personally invest $500,000 many times, $1,000,000 many times, and $2,000,000 once. I have had one Black spine surgeon, a Jamaican doctor in Jamaica, invest $500,000 and less than a handful who have invested $25,000 to $50,000 in the US. We also have the rare Black spine surgeon customer. Why is this? I touched on reasons above, but it boils down to me and my desire to overcome the challenges to increase participation with Black surgeons. Nobody owes you a helping hand to succeed. You must earn it. Many groups of people with similar desires will exhibit the classic crab in a barrel situation when there are limited opportunities. It is a factor you should understand so you develop a strong desire to overcome all situations that can hold you down. When I say overcome, I don't mean you should put yourself into places that are going to cause problems for you to overcome. I mean find ways to understand the challenges of being who you are and seek ways to succeed, knowing that you have to work harder and smarter just to be treated equally.

In general, I avoid situations where I feel I don't belong or that will not be beneficial. These are situations in which you feel defensive—where you feel you will be attacked, and so you are walking on eggshells, or you have to be combative. There are always options, so do not force any one option. There is always a better door down the hallway you can open. Just keep going. Many times, you are forced into having a single option. This is the universe at play. It then becomes the one option that gets your focus, since there is no option B. This focus will strengthen your desire to succeed no matter what obstacles you confront. Many people fail because they pursue too many options. They lack the commitment to overcome, so they fail when faced with the smallest obstacle. Some people live by jumping from option to option, without any real success, so they lose all desire for success. Avoid situations and people who make you feel defensive, as this will sap your desire and energy from emotional stress and fighting for acceptance.

As a Black entrepreneur, I am constantly on defense, never feeling like I can just be free to think and do. If I then get into situations or am around people who are going to put me even more on defense from external forces, then I could be crippled playing defense twenty-four seven. Protect your desire by developing an internal feeling that you can succeed on your own, and then carefully pick your team and environment to help you feel optimistic about yourself and your success, so you can in turn fuel your desire for success day after day. Many people get depressed by the challenges they face and by the rejection they get from people they feel should accept them. This feeling will cripple your mindset. When you experience this, develop actions that will provide you mindfulness so you can calm yourself and get control of your feelings. I achieve mindfulness by going to the gym and listening to music that uplifts my spirit. It gets even better when I go swimming right after a workout. My family, especially my children, also help me achieve mindfulness. I don't believe you will escape negative feelings and experiences, but you can prevent yourself from getting depressed by being optimistic about achieving your success. To be optimistic, you need to have clarity about what you are trying to accomplish, and you should avoid the wrong people and environments where you do not feel accepted. Never seek acceptance. Be yourself and only yourself in all situations.

DESIRE, LEADERSHIP, AND FAMILY

Growing up without a father left me with a void, so I developed a strong desire to build a family as soon as I could. Whatever the reason my father had for leaving us, I wanted to find reasons for staying and building a family when I was ready. My family is a source of desire for me to succeed financially, manage my time, and create substantive experiences. Family is not to be sacrificed for success, nor is it a sacrifice instead of success. My desire is to have a successful family and success as a leader both harmonized so there is balance. My desire for being a leader is never turned off. This means I am driven to lead in every situation. I see my family life and leadership life in the context of time periods. During different time periods, I may spend more time on my business or on my family, but I keep an internal check and observe clues to determine how well I am managing both, with the goal to achieve balance. Every day, whether I am home or traveling, I am seeking to find that balance. I don't equate balance with numerical time. I look for balance in terms of quality time. For instance, I coach my children in their sports, and when I am home, I spend quality time with them. I develop routines like making them breakfast every morning when I am home—no deviation. I see that they go to bed on time and put their clothes out the night before, so in the morning they are prepared without the stress of looking for their clothes.

Sports are definitely a focus for my kids. They know this, and my wife knows it too, so there is no room for avoiding sports. I avoided multiple sports, so they each got the chance to try different sports then choose one that they liked and were competitive in. My youngest son, Blaze, and my middle son, Kingston, are into soccer, so I enroll them in clubs and supplement their training with my personal time. My daughter, Milan, is the eldest, and she is into swimming. All of them tried golf, swimming, and soccer. Blaze was into track and field and did well. He even qualified for the Junior Olympics for south Florida in long jump when he was six years old against eight-year-olds. I remember training him to jump on the beach. I would lay down a piece of flat wood in the sand and have him run up and jump from it, landing on the soft sand so he got used to jumping and landing without fear. I spend time with all three kids in the gym to get them to understand how to use the weight room and to train their bodies, so it becomes part of their routine as they get older and more competitive. I encourage Milan to practice her turns in our pool to get her to focus on her turns, since I believe this is an opportunity to get a competitive edge. I encourage her to watch YouTube videos to develop the habit to learn on her own. I believe in laying down fundamental principles that become the foundation and infrastructure for their future, with or without me around. If they understand the value of preparation, then I hope they will find their way back to first principles and infrastructure building in all that they do, since this is what I do.

I believe in a strong foundation in mathematics for my children, just as my mother did by teaching me at home and enrolling me in after-school classes. So when they were younger, Blaze was in Kumon, and Kingston and Milan were in Mathnasium. Having formal after-school classes was something my mother did for me, and I felt it worked. There is limitation to what you can do with your time with your kids, so I find a balance between what I can teach them and what others are better at teaching them. The point is my kids know that I am investing in their education, both in school and in life, their self-development. I also share my activities and strategies with them so they can learn from my life by observing. Ultimately. I hope they will appreciate that my time is balanced between my success and theirs.

As for my wife, I try to travel with my wife on business as much as she chooses. This means I need the financial means to afford a nanny to manage our children in our absence. I love my wife, but that is not enough to sustain a long-term relationship in my experience. I think it is more important to manage your relationship, and this is also a balance between quality relationship time and time spent growing together toward new levels in life, such as in building businesses that can sustain us financially. We are both individuals, and there is no changing either of us to be someone other than who we are, so it comes down to managing our relationship to accommodate our individuality while sharing intimacy and goals.

I am brutally honest in my relationships, whether romantic, friendship, or business. I am honest in saying if we are not progressing together, I will not be able to bridge the gap to stay together, and the gap will keep widening, ultimately leading to divorce. Many people qualify their commitment to family based on how much time they spend in the home. I hear some people say they will not travel for business away from family, or they are limited in how much they invest their time into business because of family. To them, the problem is not family; they just don't feel the desire to go out and work more than forty hours or travel, so they find a reason to justify their lack of desire to succeed. I avoid setting limits on my time for success or family by ensuring that each is a priority. There are times when I am working away from my family for many days at a time, because that is what it takes to prioritize my work so that I can get to financial freedom and wealth, to have more time to be free in my decisions. Other times, I spend more time with my family, such as on scheduled family vacations.

I am training my kids to have full days of activities so that they too will use their full day. Too many people fail by living on a clock versus living to maximize their time each day. If you shut down every day by 5:00 p.m., it is unlikely that you will achieve enough success to control your life. Success comes from building relationships, and people who are successful tend to work beyond 5:00 p.m., and they get up by 5:00 a.m. They will eventually avoid counting on you for making them feel like they are chasing you to get things done. That is why we started this book with desire, because without it, you will tend to want a comfortable, predictable daily life, which will make you lose any ambition to succeed. These are the same people who later feel they have sacrificed success for family or find themselves limited in what they can experience with family or do for their family, because they are limited in their business and financial success. Family becomes a way for them to procrastinate, to avoid commitment to success. There is a saying: give a man food and easy sex, and he will give up all his ambition and drive to succeed. I know that I need financial success to afford certain experiences with my family and to have the time to spend when and how I would like with my family. So family drives my desire for financial success, and financial success comes with greater investment of my time, pursuing success and building relationships with others who also want success. I call this my desire and family circle of influence. I desire to have financial freedom to spend high quality time with my family, so I desire to work hard to achieve the means to have the financial freedom. See how desire is the start and the endpoint of the circle of influence? Without desire, you don't start, and without desire, at the end of the day or the end of an activity, you won't continue the next day or to the next activity. Desire is that fuel for daily effort, and love for my family feeds that desire to work hard.

Regardless of your unique qualifiers or disqualifiers when it comes to pursuing success at anything, I find it a must that you are always in learning mode to figure out how to make adjustments. This means you must learn from the positive outcomes as well as the negatives and disappointments, so that you acquire the desire to succeed at whatever you do and make adjustments along the way and so that you never quit. It is advantageous to seek to build your network through careful relationships that will benefit you, not distract or block you from success. Exercise a strong desire to make investments in wealth creation if you have money. It takes losing money to make money, so invest money to make money. Money is how you buy freedom and have the greatest power to make an impact. Your time is the second way, but if you can combine time and wealth, that is how you maximize your impact. Entrepreneurship is a great way to create wealth, but it is not easy for anyone, even with advantages. What really counts is your desire, resilience, and perseverance, among other positive traits you will read about throughout this book. Try not to be too busy and overlook someone who is driven to succeed and is resourceful who could be in your network. That person could be a key partner or supporter, and it goes both ways. Jeff Bezos, the founder of Amazon, needed to raise $1 million seed capital. He asked sixty-five people, but only twenty people invested between $25,000 and $50,000, each at a valuation of about $5 million. On, May 9, 2021, Amazon was worth one trillion, six hundred and sixty dollars. You will learn that complete strangers are more willing to help you because they can objectively see opportunities to work with you; they will not have preconceived ideas about your capabilities, and they will likely not be jealous.

Many people are fair-weather friends, so when the first issue comes up, they abandon you and spread the word to others to do the same. It hurts because you are loyal and intelligent and know that you would not have deserted them as they did you. Be optimistic. You will have many others who will balance out the negative people and strengthen their relationship with you, because they realize you need support, and they can see themselves in your situation. The most painful for me is when I am abandoned by the people I have helped and would sacrifice for, who then react as if I am a pariah because they think I am no longer an asset to them. There are those who always believed you were going to fail, who think you are not good enough, so they wait for signs that the day has now come for them to confirm their bias and watch you fail.

All of these realizations, though painful, should fuel your desire, as they fueled mine. Your success will be your revenge, and you might be pleasantly surprised to see your haters turn into cheerleaders. When you feel a tinge of disappointment, just remind yourself: these are the people who helped point you in the right direction, to focus you on finding another path and relying on yourself.

In 2006, when we decided to start our own medical device company, several of my spine surgeon colleagues said there were too many spine medical device companies; they wondered why I wanted to start another one. Others saw no hope in us succeeding before we even started (to them, a spine surgeon had no business starting and running a spine company), so they wouldn't entertain the idea of investing money or working with me to develop new products.

I was equally amazed that surgeons did not see that they were all customers and not business owners, and that being coddled by the sales representatives, distributors, and executives from these medical device companies created only a fleeting sense of importance. It should not have been a question of whether we would succeed or fail or whether I could make it work; it was about building our own future.

Other colleagues were concerned about fitting into medical societies and thought having ownership in a business would conflict with their society memberships. A potential investor said I had impressive credentials, but he believed I was stretched thin, and it was a matter of time before I crashed and burned. I think they all were right, but my desire to succeed meant I was going to persevere despite the hard times and failures. Luckily, the right investors decided to invest and support the creation of our products and gave us continued advice as we grew. However, the worst case happened when our main portfolio device company, SpineFrontier Inc., was accused by the Department of Justice (DOJ) of having fraudulent surgeon consulting relationships meant to induce surgeons to do surgeries as a kickback scheme. This accusation destroyed much of our investor and customer confidence. We lost many customers and investors, and hospitals shut their doors on us. This was a time when you found out who your real friends were by who was willing to stick around and be supportive. Our products are all cleared by the Food and Drug Administration (FDA), but to many doomsayers, the specter of a DOJ investigation meant we were guilty and going down, and no one wants to feel guilty by association or stay on a sinking ship. Luckily for us the pressures of the investigation forced us to change to learn how to survive and be patient. We had to play the infinite game which meant think and plan longterm. We began to appreciate the value of time and to work smart be humble and avoid wishful thinking just stay in the reality of our day to day.

It got even worse for us when in 2020 the world was hit by the COVID-19 virus pandemic. Early in the pandemic, all surgeries stopped, so we had no revenues. We had to lay off many of our employees and place some on furlough. We kept a handful of essential employees. My partner, Aditya Humad, and I did not take any salary. We spent many late nights in the office diving and swimming through the COVID-19 rough seas. We had to move fast to respond and change. This was a stressful time that should have swept us into declaring bankruptcy. We used all these adversities to fuel our desire to change and went from survival mode to thriving mode. Our desire to succeed was so strong that we had no plan B—just face the problems, learn from them, and change. We are still fighting through the DOJ investigation and the COVID-19 pandemic. It is a daily series of battles as we deal with the immediate crises while planning medium and long-term. We entered new markets to get new customers, focused on key products, and began a promotion campaign to define who we are, to stay ahead of the bad press. We are growing our revenues again, engaging investors, and seeking a strategic deal to boost us toward a targeted IPO in 2023 for one or more of our portfolio companies, under our parent company, KICVentures Group Inc. First we survive. Then we evolve to thrive.

Building a successful company or trying to rise to lead any organization is not easy, and you will not have a lot of cheerleaders until after you have succeeded. Winning leaders will get some popularity, but more will face hate. The goal should be to gain impact through success, and respect will likely be earned. Most people are intrigued by successful people only after they have succeeded, because the story then becomes interesting. Of course, we all love a success story. But even if these people had the opportunity to be a part of the journey early on, they wouldn't have been able to believe in another's potential success. This is because they can't see others succeeding any more than they can see themselves succeeding. They believe if the effort to succeed is too much for them, then it is too much for someone else as well (especially people whose capabilities they believe they know from being family, a friend, or a colleague). But take comfort in knowing that success is a personal journey, and one of the most difficult decisions on any journey is deciding to start.

All journeys must begin with the first step and with the vision of a path to a goal (your goal, not anyone else's). Just think about where we would be today if people did not go out and start new businesses or if they quit too easily. There is always a need for another good business, no matter what type. Once you start, you just need to have the desire, stand for something, find the right path, and stay on it, no matter what get-rich-quick schemes others may throw at you or what doubts they fire at you.

If you know your true situation and are moved by your desire to succeed, you'll know what you stand for. When you show success and rise above your situation, your haters will be watching you, waiting for you to fail, and looking for ways to bring you back down. Be alert to avoid mistakes. If people are talking about you, good or bad, it's because you are winning, and they are either inspired or jealous, so be courageous and persevere. It's OK to listen to others, but stay focused and be eager to learn on the job and strive to grow. I am writing this book to help you be better prepared than I was, to reach higher levels of success faster than the rate you are going, and to avoid big mistakes.

The core message is to start with your desire and nurture it so it keeps burning. Maybe it is a spark at first, so you have to work on adding fuel to create a fire. To succeed, you need commitment, and commitment needs consistency, and consistency needs desire. This book could be a spark or fuel for your desire. I recently read a quote that sums up the point of this chapter and for me as a leader: it is not our job to wake the sheep; it is our job to wake the lions. I have learned over time to direct more of my energies to helping winners win and leaders lead and less of my energy to convert losers into winners and followers into leaders. Your time is super valuable, so avoid wasting it on the wrong people and the wrong pursuits. Keep seeking knowledge and applying what you learn so you can be effective. There is enough wisdom in this book for everyone at any stage of their journey, so read on and take notes.

QUICK RECAP

Lessons on Desire:

1. It all starts with a desire to succeed. Identify and foster that desire to be fierce in your pursuit of success.
2. Set goals as steps on your path to success. It doesn't matter how small they are.
3. Celebrate your successes, big or small, because every success builds confidence.
4. Recognize your true situation before you embark on your journey.
5. Naysayers and haters are waiting for you to fail, so use them to fuel your desire for success and motivation.
6. Some people can't see your potential for success because they can't imagine their own.
7. One of the most difficult steps to take on your success journey is the first step.
8. Be at war inside yourself to be your greatest critic and cheerleader, to be in a constant, dynamic state of change and upgrading.
9. There are always changing needs for all kinds of good businesses, so don't quit on your business; keep changing.
10. Know what you stand for, be a willing learner, and don't be deterred by others.

What do you desire? Share with us.

CHAPTER 2
ESSENTIAL KEY #2
STUDY THE HISTORIES OF
SUCCESSFUL LEADERS

> Be like a shark, constantly moving, learning,
> and hunting for knowledge to survive.
> Evolve and thrive.

Successful people leave clues. Find and use them to guide your journey. It is smart to study successful people and businesses so you have examples to learn from. This is not just reading about a successful person or business once; it is studying their every move and going back to refresh, because as you learn more about success, you will be better prepared to learn more from the examples of successful businesses and people. It's like every time I watch a great movie, I notice things I did not notice the first time. This is because I have a better understanding of the story, so I can notice the small things that were not noticeable the first time I watched the movie.

I learn from anyone who has success—I mean anyone, not just the billionaire successes. I recently saw someone go from being overweight to being lean and muscular. I asked him how he did it and learned that he worked out early, lifting weights then doing cardio, all while fasting, so he burned fat. During the day, he eats mostly fish and limited amounts of carbohydrates, no more than seventy-five grams. The next day, I thought about what he said, and I then went back to what I learned in medical school and what is new to get the knowledge. I learned that it is more complex than what he said, but he gave me the start to go learn more. For example, I do not have to fast right before my workout. I fast overnight at least twelve to sixteen hours, but I need a great workout with energy, so I drink a smoothie with carbohydrates from the vegetables and oats I mix in. You will lose weight by doing high-impact interval training, which keeps your heart rate at least 70–80 percent of your maximum heart rate (subtract your age from 220). Dieting will do the rest by managing your calorie intake and avoiding sugar and bad carbohydrates. This is what I mean. As you succeed, you are better able to extract value from successful people and what you can learn on your own, so you are never at the point where you stop thirsting to learn. I use the word *thirsting* because as you use the knowledge you gained, you will feel like you are drying out, and you will need more knowledge to quench your thirst. Ever notice how dry ground sucks up even the tiniest raindrops?

I make every successful person a mentor, so I elevate them to teacher status, and I am their student. Someone told me his mentors were too busy for him. My answer was my mentors are not just people who I can talk with or who are even alive. Some mentors teach you not just with their words; they are people you want to associate with, so you feed off their energy and get into their circle, increasing your standards and your value measured against theirs. When you show an eagerness to learn, a mentor may be someone who connects you to someone or an opportunity because they saw your potential and love your attitude. Attitude determines your altitude because of the help people will give you to help you advance.

So my mentors come from all sources: real life, books, movies, social media, and documentaries, to just name a few. I love to watch reruns of History Channel's *The Men Who Built America.* It never gets stale, watching how the giants of industry like Andrew Carnegie, John D. Rockefeller, Cornelius Vanderbilt, Henry Ford, and J. P. Morgan built the foundation for America's industrial growth. I was further amazed to learn how they were simple men; most of them were from humble beginnings. They all exhibited the same drive and tenacity to grow their individual companies. We all should be compelled to acquire many of the traits they exhibited. I was equally amazed when I learned that the idea of an electric car has been around since the 1800s, long before Elon Musk and Tesla. Trailblazers in Hungary, the Netherlands, and the US created the first small-scale electric cars. In 1890, William Morrison, a chemist in Des Moines, Iowa, developed a six-passenger vehicle capable of fourteen miles per hour, which helped spark interest in electric vehicles. Today, companies led by Tesla are relearning about electric cars and innovating blazing new paths. I imagine if you look far back in history, you might just rediscover a great idea whose time has come.

Studying successful entrepreneurs will help you become a motivated entrepreneur. Keep referring to their stories to keep your desire to succeed burning. Most successful entrepreneurs I know of had to transform themselves to become successful. Great entrepreneurs can emerge at any stage of their lives, if they develop the right traits and implement them. Don't be intimidated into thinking you need a business degree and high grade-point average to succeed. Don't think you need people to validate your abilities. Any form of self-improvement, such as advanced education, will give you formal preparation to supplement your knowledge, which could improve your ability to lead any organization but especially those that require formal blueprints to capitalize on opportunities. I once went to a fundraising event and talked to one of the honorees and his wife. I walked them to the valet because I was so inspired by his story. He left me with the thought that he had been at the bottom of his class, thought to be the troublemaker and someone who would not amount to much. He founded a company that employs former prisoners and has grown that company successfully. He advises me to look for leaders who might not seem to fit in with the status quo or who been branded as failures but who have the drive to succeed and are trainable. If you search among my employees over the years, you will see that I have followed his advice in many cases within KICVentures' employee pool.

The people who graduate at the top of their classes, for example, feel they have a lot of options and tend to go with the sure thing, such as chasing high-paying jobs versus building long-term with a company or starting a company. They have the talents and the credentials and a clear path to success if they stay the course and fit in, but they are valuable to any organization, so they play the game to increase their salaries and titles rather than going out to try to build a company as an equity owner, to find personal and financial freedom. Rising among the ranks of an organization to find financial success is only one path. Many great success stories did not follow a safe path within a corporation.

Mark Zuckerberg left Harvard to start Facebook, now valued at over $500 billion, while many thought he was too young to run the company when it was announced Facebook was going public, leading up to its IPO. He was not looking to fit in; he followed his vision and proved himself and succeeded in changing the world.

Warren Buffett, after graduating from Columbia Business School, did not take the traditional route to work in Manhattan on Wall Street. He went to Omaha, Nebraska, and built an investment partnership, which positioned him to look for opportunities. He found one when he bought stocks in Berkshire Hathaway, a textile manufacturing company, which he later took control of in 1965. Berkshire Hathaway is now one of the most successful investment firms in the world.

Amazon founder Jeff Bezos was born to a teenage mother but did well for himself as a student, graduating from Princeton University.

He wanted to build his own firm, so he left a safe job working in a hedge fund company and took a three-week course in selling books before he started his internet company, originally called Cadabra, in July 1994. He later renamed it Amazon and rose to become the richest man in the world. Amazon has diversified into owning many businesses, changing the way the world purchases products from retail stores in a mall to online with the click of a keypad.

In 1984, Oprah Winfrey took over a little-known talk show in Chicago and turned it into one of the most successful daytime talk shows in history. Oprah went on to establish her own Oprah Winfrey Network.

In 1980, Robert with his wife, Sheila Johnson, launched Black Entertainment Television (BET), which would eventually become a $3 billion company from a $15,000 loan. BET, a cable network, was created for an African American audience and soon became hugely popular, later listed on the New York Stock Exchange and making history as the first African American–owned company to do so. In 2001, Robert Johnson sold BET to Viacom for a reported $3 billion, becoming the first African American billionaire. Although he held a master's in international affairs, his jobs in communications media are what eventually exposed him to the cable network opportunity, which he was hungry enough to pursue.

So if you want to be successful, learn from successful people like these; study them and emulate them, and you too will learn to find a way to succeed. Smart people know this, to learn from others rather than to only learn from their own experiences. The examples I gave show that to get great success, you must be willing to go it alone to be different. Talent is equally distributed throughout the world, but taking advantage of opportunities, no matter how small, is up to you, no matter where you were born. Learning and taking advantage of opportunities is the way to financial freedom. People who are given a lot of support, easily fit in, and are validated by others are often too afraid of disrupting the status quo to reach for something new or better. They may also be unwilling to dedicate the time it takes to building great success because this may take them away from the people they are most comfortable with in their lives. Instead, they choose to spend time on others, to be a good friend rather than working toward their own success, which risks outgrowing their friends. If you set high personal goals and dedicate yourself to reach them, while surrounding yourself with leaders who push you to reach your greatest potential, you won't just feel the need to fit in, as you will be focused on reaching your goals, learning, changing along the way, and building new networks of friends. If you want to fit in, do so with people who are highly successful, and you will become the next highly successful person in the group.

Whether you have the credentials or not, and even if you didn't graduate from high school or college, if you have experienced adversity or realize you might not make the grade working in a standard corporate environment, you may not make it to the top. You might want to take that step to start gaining life and industry experience, to start your own business, or to look for a start-up and jump on board. Or better yet, hitch your wagon to an entrepreneur you admire and believe will succeed, learning from them to eventually establish your own success, or get to success alongside them and share in the bounty. Many millionaires and billionaires got their wealth from working with other millionaires and billionaires, so join a successful team if you don't want to go out on your own and build one. The story goes like this: if you hang around millionaires, you will become the next millionaire or billionaire. So start with gaining the knowledge you need for success, and the best place to start, to keep refreshing yourself, is studying successful people and associating with them to bring them value. Bill Gates's high school friend became a multibillionaire after taking over Microsoft as CEO. He was rich enough to buy the Los Angeles Clippers National Basketball Association (NBA) team for over $1 billion. So you can become successful working to help someone else succeed.

CREATE STRENGTHS OUT
OF WEAKNESSES

If you take the step to become an entrepreneur, or if you are in a company that fosters your entrepreneurial spirit and you want a leadership role, it is imperative that you look to transform your weaknesses into strengths. One of the best ways to do this is to transform your habits, your environment, and the people around you. People who overlooked you, criticized you, or doubted your abilities might have had valid reasons. They were not doing it in your best interest, but that does not mean everything they said about you was untrue.

When I came to the US, my Jamaican accent was quite thick, and I was a poor writer. I was uncomfortable raising my hand to answer questions, because my reply was often misunderstood, and I had to repeat the answer, which diminished the sense that I was saying something of substance. This is true for anyone; communication is important to gain respect. People will judge you as soon as you open your mouth to speak. My first paper as a freshman at Columbia College was so poorly written the professor asked me to stay behind to discuss how badly it was written and what my plan was to improve drastically.

Knowing these two weaknesses, I began to read more, I sought help from a classmate to proofread my papers and guide me in becoming a better writer, I took a speech and communications class, and I listened keenly to great speakers like Jesse Jackson, Malcolm X, Martin Luther King, and Marcus Garvey. I knew if I wanted to be transformed and become a transformational leader one day, I had to become better at writing and speaking.

At this time in my life, I was also not the best morning person. Neither was I the most prompt at getting things done. I knew early on I wanted to become an effective leader, so I had to develop better habits in leading myself first. I admired other people who had great personal traits, and I wanted to be like them. In college, I would plan to get up early but instead hit the snooze button until I had no time to spare before rushing to get where I needed to go.

I was also the worst at getting assignments done ahead of time. I would wait until the night before a paper was due, then spend all night working on it. I am describing the habit of procrastination, putting things off, which is a killer of success. One moment of procrastination could cost you over a month of time or a lifetime from a missed opportunity. The problem was feeling like my back was against the wall because of lost time seemed to work for me, giving me moments of intense focus and drive through high school, and it seemed to be working for me now in college, but it was a bad habit, and I knew it, so I recognized it had to change. Over the years, I've shaped myself to be an early riser, to stop snoozing the clock, and to get up with a sense of purpose, ready to get going and generating desire and intense focus without deadlines. I have to be honest: some mornings, I do snooze the clock once or twice, but I am getting up after the second snooze. I learned to hold myself accountable for improving my habits, getting things done, setting schedules, and testing myself to see how much better I could become as I developed the traits of the successful people I read about. However, it is hard to always be so wound up and regimented every day, so the more you plan ahead and take care of what needs to be done, the fewer urgent matters you'll have that put you in crisis mode.

To be effective, I need to exercise and feel like I am achieving things. These two feelings make me feel in control, so there's less stress on my mind and spirit. Follow your inner feelings and do what makes you happy, but avoid putting yourself in crisis mode by procrastinating. We will perform our best and be happiest when we spend most of our time on accomplishing important things without urgency by planning ahead. This is what Stephen Covey describes as living in quadrant two. Avoid quadrant one with urgent and important matters, which are crises.

You might relate to my experiences. Some of us never change. It's how we're formed, how we've been, and how we may always be. But for me, this all changed when I decided I wanted to be a successful entrepreneur and build wealth and impact as a transformational leader. I wanted to achieve the mogul status of some of the business greats, become influential, and impact the world (recall my vision?). As I studied them, I realized I must transform my habits. I now set my clock to get up no later than 6:30 every morning, no matter what, but if my schedule changes, I get up much earlier. It does not matter if it is a weekday or weekend; having a fixed schedule forced me to develop this habit. I used to go to the gym every morning by six o'clock for an hour workout, but now I take mornings to focus on my children, to make breakfast with them, help as they get set for the day, and bring them to school. This is my special time with my children, and especially as I travel so much, it's important for bonding. My gym time can be morning or evening or when I am traveling, and gym time is a priority. I exercise at least three days during the week. I prefer going to the gym before 6:00 a.m. for an hour, as it does not interfere with my day schedule. If you are not a morning person, that is OK since your body works even better between 2:00 and 6:00 p.m. The more successful I become, the more flexibility in my workout schedule.

The next habit I learned to adopt was getting things done and off my plate immediately, so they didn't pile up on me. All successful people seem to be very effective with their time and getting things done, building more and more (not accomplishing less) as they succeed. I knew I needed to develop this habit to get more things done in a shorter time span, so I could take on more, learn more, build more companies, and be there for my relationships. People know if I say I am going to do something, I do it, and I want to be done with it as quickly as possible. The idea is to not carry around other people's stuff on your back. You want to get it off and onto their backs to free up your mind, so you don't have the responsibility weighing you down. If you bury your head in the sand, you darn well know that this issue is not going away, and at some point, you'll come up with excuses as to why it took you so long to do it, which leads to more stress and problems.

I think it's more difficult not getting things done, coming up with excuses, and dealing with the fallout. It is so much easier to get it done, do a great job, and not have to worry about the consequences of not getting the job done. I spent my Thanksgiving night writing this chapter because I gave my staff a deadline—that I would be done writing all the chapters by Saturday morning. I had this chapter to write so that the next day, I could focus on other chapters and still make time for my family. I can put off writing this chapter as long as I want, but I have other people who are editing this book with me, and I need to deliver on my promise at some point, so I might as well get it done now and get it done well. This all starts with focus and a decision to do it.

Great entrepreneurs are tenacious. They are all in and do not see failure as the end but just a lesson. Are you tenacious? By studying real-life situations, especially ones you can relate to, you might develop a road map for how you will become more tenacious and hang in there like all successful people do, and eventually, your tenacity will pay off. Once you have developed that trait and transformed yourself, other traits will rub off on you if you continue to study successful entrepreneurs. You can have their successes to reference, like a library of stories, when you find yourself in similar circumstances or when speaking to your team or an audience you want to motivate or convince. So look for these kinds of business experiences to store in your heart and mind. You can learn and benefit from others who have been successful in a similar regard.

BE INSPIRED BY LEADERSHIP ROLE MODELS

Look through the mirror, look past your reflection, and look back into history to study great entrepreneurs and learn from them. Look even closer at the great entrepreneurs who are still alive. Read their biographies or even write to them to ask them questions. Being that I want to be a leader, I am always studying effective influencers. One of the leaders I admire most, Marcus Mosiah Garvey Jr., was born in the tiny seaside town of Saint Ann's Bay, Jamaica, in 1887, eventually immigrating to the United States to continue to build the United Negro Improvement Association (UNIA). Saint Ann's Bay is just a few miles along the coast line west of Buff Bay, where I was born. I first read his biography when I was a sophomore at Columbia University and was immediately struck by the enormity of his vision, to raise money from individuals to build a fleet of steamships. He called the company the Black Star Line, with the intention of doing business between Africa and the Caribbean and the US. At one point, he owned multiple businesses in New York City, employing people of color. He had more than six million members of his UNIA organization worldwide, across dozens of countries.

How amazing is it that in an era without the internet, he could compile such a mass of people for the same goal? He would boldly take his followers, thousands and thousands strong, and march down the streets of Harlem to show confidence and draw attention to his Black nationalism and Pan-Africanism movement. He believed in political power for Black people and self-empowerment through entrepreneurship and proved he could make a difference in this way. Unfortunately, he overlooked the sinister practice of the Federal Bureau of Investigation (FBI) and Edgar Hoover, the leader at the time, to take down potentially disruptive Black leaders. Marcus Garvey was eventually accused of wire fraud, raising money without the prerequisite protocols, and deported back to Jamaica, where he was not able to garner the same respect from his fellow Jamaicans and from previous followers, who saw him as tarnished. He tried and failed at a political career in Jamaica, became impoverished, and died in England.

But as we know, time heals, and he was ultimately recognized in

America and Jamaica as a fierce Black leader and entrepreneur and became the first national hero back home in Jamaica. Generations later, I am one of his admirers and a student of his vision of political and economic self-improvement for Black people everywhere. It's just no longer the time to march and beg for racial equality anymore; we must make ourselves equal through results of our hard work, especially entrepreneurship. I think he would be pleased with my drive to succeed at all costs and to know that I studied his strengths and weaknesses, his successes and failures, and am trying to find ways to achieve a high level of economic empowerment for others (Blacks and others). I am engaged in Jamaica at the same time I am engaged in the world at large, through my many companies and through the internet as a motivational leader, sharing the message of political and economic self-improvement. The ultimate similarity is in the current Federal Department of Justice investigation I am defending. I learned to not follow Marcus and represent myself, instead to be humble and seek the best legal representation. I hope to successfully defend the allegations.

While my successes are yet to be determined, I am focused on pursuing my vision to be impactful in my way.

This chapter will repeat the essential key: we must decide to learn from others who have succeeded in life and business. If you make the same mistakes over and over, and you still think you know it all, you will likely fail or underachieve, and no one will be moved to help you when you need it. And remember, everyone needs help to succeed at some point. If you learn from your mistakes and humbly seek knowledge, you will become smarter, and humility attracts mentors. If you learn from other people's mistakes and adopt the habits of highly successful people, you will become smarter, be successful, and gain similar results.

It is important to identify role models, people you can look up to and emulate. They may be people from history who literally changed the world and shaped the way we live due to their foresight and innovation. They may be contemporary people who are constantly in the news, the big players of our day and age who chase (and achieve) success. Or they could be other people in your company who challenge you and approach life with an attitude and spirit that you admire. It is key to learn how to follow a leader before you become one or ask people to follow you. As a leader, I also serve as a follower of my own leadership, by doing and leading from the front, being an employee like everyone else, getting things done, being dependable, and not delegating like managers do. As a leader, I build teams and ensure everyone can deliver on their responsibilities, so we are all followers, and we are all leaders at the same time. In plain language, I build leaders, not followers. Even if you are following me, it is likely that you will find yourself leading somewhere in your life from the lessons you learn from this book and me.

By identifying successful people around you, it becomes easier to look at the common traits they exhibit. Observe their management styles, how they act in high-stress situations, how they treat the lowest people they encounter, like the janitorial staff. What is it that you admire about them, and how can you emulate that trait? As a leader, learn humility and demonstrate it in how you treat people below you on the ladder. This will keep you grounded, so you too can look up to others and learn how to get better, simultaneously helping those below you improve. I believe leaders should judge themselves by how they treat the lowest-level people in their organization or citizens in their country. Mentor the highest performers. You should be nurturing your successors, ensuring the future success and sustainability of your family tree, organization, or business.

There is value in identifying what you want to learn from others. Personally, I am constantly thinking about how I can be a better entrepreneur, leader, and businessman, as well as making the time to be a great family man. To do this, I need to honestly and objectively look at my weaknesses. I want to be a better CEO every day. I pinpoint my weaknesses and then find others who are strong in those areas to learn from. If they can overcome a weakness, I know that I can as well. I am always trying to transform myself by learning from my successes and failures, at the same time studying the traits of others.

Look at successful leaders both in and out of your industry. By examining effective companies within your industry, you can analyze their strategies and see how your firm compares. You will likely have multiple similarities, so it may be easier to take what they are doing and do it better. By studying successful companies outside of your industry, you gain a fresh perspective and a new approach, which can inspire you to be more creative and unique within your industry. It is amazing how far a company can advance by applying strategies from a different field. It's valuable to learn from people who are like you, but it's also important to study people who are not like you. Focus on people above owning things, and you will do fine as a servant leader.

You are never too old to learn. Read books by successful people and allow their journeys to inspire your own. Travel to new places and meet entrepreneurs from different cultures; allow them to broaden your worldview and aspire to achieve their level of success in your own organization. Go to conferences, meet successful people, and get to know them. Successful people like to tell their stories, so engage them in deep conversations; they will enjoy seeing you as an interested student of success. Audit conferences attended by successful people and stay up to date on what the leaders of the industry are doing, so you can be on top of the game.

Join a networking group and have an open mind as you meet others with varying levels of success. Remember, your success will be affected by the people you associate with in your business pursuits, so choose to be with people who will help drive you or who are more successful than you are in areas you need help with; they can guide you to grow faster and give you a support network to reference in times of need. If you associate with people below your level, you will be their source of help, and they will drag you down, even if they are your longtime friend from when you were in diapers together. They just will not be able to help you progress, because they don't have the knowledge or means beyond yours (plus, people who are close to you or who know you are easily prone to jealousy and will sabotage rather than support).

So it's best to find mentors and successful people you can learn from and be comfortable with going it alone. I had a ninety-three-year-old patient, Lou, who lived on Palm Beach Island. In 2008, he agreed to act as my mentor, when I was just trying to get settled in my practice as an orthopedic spine surgeon and *doctorpreneur* in West Palm Beach. I remember the story he told me. When he was forty-five years old, he had created enough wealth to retire from his real estate investments. He also talked about how much more money he could have made when he looked at where New York City real estate had come since he retired, witnessing the success of his friend who continued to invest and who now owned billions of dollars of New York City real estate. But he was also very satisfied with his life and the trips he took with his wife before she died. However, I did get the feeling he had too much time to sit around, and he would still dabble in buying and renovating condos in his building to stay busy. I learned my retirement plan from him, and I know it will not be sitting around in Palm Beach, watching time creep by. I will be investing in developing businesses and mentoring young entrepreneurs, and I definitely will not have regrets. Thank you, Lou.

Lou made sure he booked lunch for us every Wednesday. I studied how generous he was with tipping, and that became a big thing for me regarding how you treat people. Lou would tip everyone very generously and discreetly in cash. He made sure he asked for the same people every time we went to a restaurant, and they were glad to oblige. He had the biggest grin of satisfaction whenever he made someone happy by giving. He probably felt he got the best of the exchange.

So become a student of history and successful people, for this will keep you humble, increase your knowledge, and build a foundation for success. Allow yourself to absorb their characteristics and mindset, and one day, you too will be transformed into a leader for others to emulate.

ACTIONS OF A GREAT LEADER

I want to conclude by supplying a short list of the actions I see leaders embody to be effective. Over the years, I've observed these actions as essential to a leader's success, so I foster them for myself and those I mentor. Before listing these essential actions, I will list the character traits I believe are also important. By the way, it takes a lifetime to build your character. As you may have noticed, in my case, it has been a journey of learning from others and changing my bad habits as I aspired to be a better leader of myself and others through example. If you stop learning, you will stop being effective in leading yourself and others. Here are a few of my character traits for leaders. I believe leaders should aspire to be family oriented, driven, disciplined, resilient, determined, hardworking, resourceful, inspirational, confident, magnetic, optimistic, intelligent, credible, visionary, fair, humble, caring, forgiving, honest, truthful, active listeners, and have 100 percent integrity. Below are the actions I see successful leaders take:

- *Ownership.* Leaders must take full ownership of their vision. This means taking absolute responsibility for completing their tasks, including the failure or success of a given project. People who are not leaders don't take full ownership. Sure, they're happy to be involved in the process of completing tasks as single transactions, but they don't take full responsibility for the success or failure of the bigger goal.

- *Being all in.* People can sense whether or not their leader is all in. Leaders must be fully invested in their goals to see them accomplished. Giving anything less than everything is simply not enough and is a bad signal to your team, investors, and customers.
- *Intelligence.* Leaders must build intelligence through reading and analyzing situations from which they can learn how to deploy intelligence, meaning they need the ability to understand the current industry climate in different scenarios and environments in all their complexity. They must build the intelligence through gathering and analyzing data so they can process new information rapidly, adjust their business practices and leadership accordingly, and be able to answer pressing questions and give solutions to problems. Don't confuse this intelligence with test-taking intelligence and memorization or what you were born with, such as your IQ. I mean more common sense and being able to quickly analyze and organize your options, acting on the best one, using data to manage your results. A lot of intelligence comes from your adversity quotient (AQ)—how much adversity you have encountered and what you have learned.
- *Knowledge.* Having a solid knowledge base is fundamental to leadership and intelligence, so read a lot. Great leaders, when they have all the right information, are able to make quick, calculated decisions in the best interest of the company. Therefore, great leaders remain humble, surrounding themselves with people they can learn from. Mistakes are learning opportunities.
- *Desire for success.* Great leaders must find ways to develop and build their desire to succeed. For leaders to get up every day and lead by example, they must have an intense and disciplined desire to succeed, or they will simply lose their drive over time, or when faced with a small obstacle,

they will quit to find easier opportunities. Great leaders have zero tolerance for lazy people who will not help them meet their goals and achieve success. Whereas those who are merely comfortable as managers might feel the sting of not obtaining success, they may not hold the critical view a leader does in not achieving the opportunity at hand. The title of leader is not as important as the desire to gain the trust of the people they lead.

- *Mentorship.* Great leaders seek to develop the skills and abilities of people on their team and in their organization, with the intention of grooming a potential successor. This is crucial to serve as the sustainability of a leader's goals. Leaders must realize how crucial they are in the process of teaching those around them how to succeed, therefore putting in place a succession plan for mentees to help build the company, feel a sense of ownership, and be ready to become more of a full-time mentor and less of an operator or a boss.

What is the most important lesson you've learned from studying a mentor? Share with us.

QUICK RECAP

Lessons on Studying Successful People:

1. Learn from studying great successes to build your library of success stories.
2. Get experience and learn from others to give you an edge.
3. Create strengths out of your weaknesses by transforming your weak habits into strong ones.
4. Develop tenacity, knowing failure is a great teacher and determination leads to success.

5. Find role models from history and use their greatness as inspiration.

6. Identify successful people around you and emulate their traits.

7. Study successful companies, both inside and outside of your industry, for fresh approaches.

8. Read, travel, have conversations, take classes, and network to be a lifelong learner on the job, keeping yourself open to new perspectives.

9. Believe you are destined to succeed, but also be determined so you breed confidence.

10. Anticipate or quickly recognize the next great thing. Even better, know what must happen next and prepare for it.

CHAPTER 3
ESSENTIAL KEY #3

FOCUS ON BUILDING A WORKING
TEAM WITH WINNERS

*If you want to win, identify talented people with
the right attitude and build a working team.*

This is a chapter to pay attention to because team building is necessary for success both at home and in business. Grade A leaders hire A people and empower them to be at their greatest for the team. Show me a winning team, and I'll show you a successful leader of a team of talented winners dedicated to one another and the success of the team, without sacrificing personal success. Winning teams create the opportunity for greater individual successes. There is little success if you don't have people with the ability to succeed or if you are not able to get successful people to work together. So if asked whether you prefer to win or lose, the expected answer should be to win. But building a winning team does not start with a focus on winning; it should start with building a team of winners who want to win by working together. Leaders have to emerge that will lead by example, and systems and processes must be put in place to ensure a culture exists for the team members to perform at their best, even when you add or subtract players or change leadership. If you are trying to build a winning team, how do you know when you have one? In a contest, one team wins, but does that make them a winning team? Can that team win again and again, every time they compete? One day later? One month later? What about every day?

When you win, do you know why? How about when you lose? Even when the team wins a competition, can they stay together? Building a winning team should be about confidence in the culture and systems so that the team can win over and over again, regardless of the players who come and go. Even in sports, when you have a winning team, you should be thinking dynasty since there is no guarantee you will win in any given year. Build a team that can win every year. Some teams have not won a championship in over fifty years, so build a team that can win year after year and increase your odds of winning in any given year. Often, due to pride, unforeseen circumstances, or time, a team that wins a competition dismantles itself and no longer remains a team, so they won but don't see winning as a habit that leads to greatness and legacy. Focus on hiring winners who want to win over and over again and who then want to be coached to work together and follow the plans that will lead to wins. Every team would like to win, but many teams only focus on winning as a desire. I think there is a natural uneasiness within a team when individual players strive to just win rather than wanting to win together. I often see the top teams in a league all bunched up together with similar records, maybe a few points difference, because they are all focused on simply winning, whereas winning teams have one or more great players who lead by example and get the team to work together, with a strong desire to give their best individual efforts. Teams that build dynasties focus on building a winning culture with the right leadership, who implements systems and processes. It's the old saying: systems fail, not people. Next is to assemble winners with the right winning attitude. Hiring for attitude and culture fit is key to identifying winners. Someone who you don't see as a fit might be a superstar in another team where they fit, and vice versa. Next is to teach the team to work together and how to win together around one or more superstars who set the winning standard for performance on and off the field. Michael Jordan was successful in this system; they had a great coach, and they assembled the right players for the right roles and had a culture for teamwork. Michael Jordan and Scottie Pippen set the standard for winning and led by example.

The experiences of real life are not part of a season, with a referee and rules and a trophy that says you won, but many lessons can be used from sports teams. I focus more on building a working team of talented people, with a few superstars who enjoy collaborating, setting goals, studying our industry, measuring their improvements, obsessing over our customers, and scheduling critical meetings rather than going it alone. As a leader, I ensure I lead by example and coach to help each team member perform at their best, for themselves and the team. I do this by inspiring the team to think toward a big goal, with daily accounting of the goals to get us there, and I encourage each person to see the value in what they contribute. Teams focused more on individualism often have members who don't get along, but they tolerate each other because the goal is not too far into the future and doesn't require a long-term commitment. Soon afterward, they can hardly wait to move to another team. The competition will eventually build a better team and adjust to beat the winning team, while the winning team is unlikely to make the needed changes and work consistently hard enough to keep winning (which is harder to do than trying to work together as a team). People on any team focused on winning over working together will in time see the grass is greener somewhere else, versus watering the grass to be greener day by day. A winning team will have members who come together to work together and therefore win together.

If you are a leader who puts winning ahead of the team working best together, you risk building a culture that is about your ambition, and you are putting pressure on individuals to hit individual goals, and thus they become afraid of making mistakes (which can sometimes cause the team to lose), and you might overlook the details that could disrupt the team spirit. You might also be telling your superstars to win at all costs, and because they think they have the ability to carry the team and get your favor, they try to do it all, and this sacrifices teamwork. Teams sometimes do win with this formula. In this scenario, I usually give credit to a leader who is a great motivator and disciplinarian, who focuses on details and is hands-on. Winning does have a way of building winners and inspiring confidence in a team to want to keep winning. This is a risky approach and leads to a high turnover rate and poor resilience and resourcefulness, which are important traits to overcome obstacles in the way of winning. When the team is not working well together and following the systems, decisions start to seem arbitrary, and players start to think more about protecting themselves.

During my senior year in college, our soccer team was undefeated halfway through the season. We thought we were invincible. I even had a conversation with the coach about what it would take to be selected for the All-American team. Others were also thinking about individual accolades if we continued to win. We never expected what happened next: we started to lose, game after game. We were not prepared for losing and did not make adjustments. We were built to be a winning machine with individual performances, and when the machine was broken, we did not know individually or as a team how to make it work again. Winning games had been in our culture since training camp, and we had not planned how we would adjust to losing, and we never came together as a team with a clear system to follow. We were not glued together as a working team; we were individuals driven to win, so we won nothing that year. It is critical to bring winners together to build a winning team, but the focus should be first on getting the members, including the winners, to work together, and the individual accolades will come. When the tide rises, all boats rise.

Because of my individual performance, I was named the Ivy League Player of the Year. I appreciated the honor and am grateful to every coach who voted for me, but I wish I could let them know now that my disappointment in getting that award after our team imploded was one of the great motivators for how much I value team building today. It is one of the reasons why I try to get the best out of each person and encourage everyone to consistently work hard as a contributing member of the team, to prepare for the mistakes, to be nimble, to be hands-on, and to do the job, because we depend on each and every person. I teach people to be selfless, to always look for reasons to be of help, and that means being dependable with each hour of the day. I ask everyone to do their job as urgently as possible in getting across the finish line, because we all depend on them closing out their individual responsibilities. Bottom line, we want to win, but we must focus on being a great team, where everyone becomes great at their individual roles then comes together and collaborates and executes as a team on even the smallest project. When you start with winners and teach them how to win as a team, then teamwork consistently results in winning, and the dream happens. During a game or in business, the coach cannot be the players, and so you want players to also be leaders of themselves and one another so they can make adjustments that will benefit the team.

At KICVentures, we rely on leaders leading by example. We embrace failures and successes because successes are building blocks for taking on more ambitious tasks, while failures unite us and keep us humble to learn and make changes in the form of innovation. But we also don't accept letting the team down when they depend on us to get the job done. Easy or quick success can lead to complacency and confusion among a team, since there are many factors behind succeeding, but people like to find answers and take credit. We celebrate our successes, and your team should too. Celebrate even the small successes for team appreciation, but avoid spectacular goals that are all-or-nothing missions. Instead, build a working team that will continuously set manageable goals and succeed. Even if you are succeeding, make time to analyze your team's strengths and weaknesses and prepare them for managing failures as well as successes.

ARE YOU AT WAR, OR IS IT PEACETIME?

In approaching team building, I sometimes think of what I would do if I were building an army. Next, I think of what the army is going to be doing. Is it being built to fight a war that is happening now that threatens our very existence, or is it being built to take over other companies and increase our market share? Should we build it to do both but split it into different forces? Do I need an elite special forces team that is nimble and easily deployable, with intense focus and execution skills? If the team is small and has limited resources, should we deploy all our resources at one target at a time?

The answer is yes to all the above. War is a great metaphor for team building. If you are paranoid when it comes to the fear of failure, then imagine you are at war and your very existence is being threatened, so you cannot fail, even if you lose a few battles.

Build a team to go on the offensive because the best defense is a great offense. For the team to succeed in defending the company from threats and to gain market share, the members must work well together and adjust to urgent matters. Strong rhetoric will motivate, but if your team consists of lots of individuals making individual decisions, albeit with good intentions, you do not have a working team, and chances of success are slim. In addition to building a working team, you as the CEO must recognize the difference between fighting a war to defend your company and being at peace and aiming to expand the business and strengthen your market position. This recognition must be communicated to the team in speech and action. The wartime team has to be given strict projects to execute with precision and urgency, and you must be hands-on and fully informed. There is no wiggle room for individual creativity and initiative. Time is of the essence; each option has to be quickly explored, and real-time communication up and down the chain of command must be happening. The message is follow the script, communicate, and execute the mission; otherwise, you get isolated and killed, and the team and the company will follow in death.

The team has to have core members who embody the mission and stick together, because quick decisions about who stays or gets fired from the team are constantly shifting who is on the team and why. Keeping the team together is challenging when changes are happening so fast. I have hired employees and let them go within days of them starting. I have had others who started and did very well but shortly thereafter fell short, and I quickly recognized that they were great for the stage they came in, but after they got us to the next stage, they could not perform at the next level, so I had to let them go. Your team is as strong as the weakest link, so you must bring on strong players, and you cannot hesitate in a time of war to let go of someone who is weak. Make no mistake: losing team members is a major loss; consider the time you invested in hiring, training, and integrating that individual into the team.

Wartime teams must have thick skin, but it is up to the leader to be there to keep the team together emotionally when personal conflicts appear; leaders must act quickly to use those conflicts to either make changes to the membership or seize the opportunity to adjust your expectations. I am always looking at the managers first whenever there is an issue that threatens the team working together. I have been known to fire managers when they report problems with team members, because I conclude that they created the environment in the first place and that the conflict became inevitable because of their lack of leadership, not because of an individual's failure. I remind them that systems fail, not just people, but I also look to see if we have the right people in the system.

One of my project managers, I will call her Mary, is disliked by many of my staff because she is hands-on in her management style, but our culture likes to empower each person to have more latitude and less hands-on management. I created a special forces team to oversee projects that other people are working on. I placed Mary in charge because she is great when given a directive, and she would get specific things done and report back immediately. This more often than not conflicts with the regular team members' timeline and their sense of control. They take it out on my project manager, who is like a pit bull and does not stop, even though she might feel slighted by personal feelings against her. She is emboldened by her repeated success, so she learned to decrease the collateral personality damage to the team, but she is also reassured by me stepping in to reinforce her usefulness, and results speak the loudest in the end anyway. Because she stirs up the waters, I have had the opportunity to address underperforming employees who were hiding beneath the surface. However, over time, conflicts were preventing us from becoming a working team, and I felt Mary had become a source of conflict, so she was relieved of the position and left the company. Having a working team where you trust the members and they follow the processes means you have strong individual team members who will execute during the stress of wartime when you have little room for mistakes.

In peacetime, I still keep the feeling that we are at war, but I am more tolerant of individual creativity that is shared with the team, and I focus on building systems and mentoring the future team leaders. We are more liberal with growing the team and exploring relationships outside the company to work with us internally. We look to expand our physical footprint, acquire new companies, and integrate new expertise; during wartime, the task dictates the person we throw at it. The key, in war or peace, is to build a working team and maintain that relationship between the team members and you, the CEO. They should know your vision of the big picture, so communication needs to be frequent and flow freely to all who are affected by decisions; the team must be ready to respond the moment you call on them to go to war for the company, to stay alive or expand.

HOW TO CREATE A WORKING TEAM THAT WILL SUCCEED

After you have identified your desire and built the team, you must then articulate the vision to team members to help them see the big picture, understand how they fit in, and determine what ownership and rewards there will be for everyone if the team succeeds. This will prepare everyone for how much work, time, and sacrifice will be needed to justify the rewards that may lie ahead. You must also decide what you stand for and not just what products you are going to sell. Products that are hot today are obsolete tomorrow, so build a team that will be nimble and competent.

Establish a set of principles to dedicate your team to so they have a high level of employee satisfaction, or what I like to call the togetherness quotient (TQ). Here are five principles by which your wartime and peacetime teams will be hired and trained and how they will operate together:

The first principle is communication. Everyone who works with me knows that I will answer any phone call at any time, that there are no stupid questions, and that I am brutally honest and won't pull any punches (and neither should they). We have regularly scheduled chalkboarding or online sessions to discuss every new strategy, direction, and decision that requires teams to work together. Currently, my executive strategy team meets with me from 8:15 to 9:00 a.m. every morning online, except Wednesdays, when the whole company meets with me from 8:30 to 9:00 a.m. All these meetings are on a Microsoft team's application. We want everyone to be in the know. Communication is the cornerstone to productivity, which is why we aim for 100 percent transparency within our organization. During tough times, we weather the storm openly and honestly; I see this period as an opportunity for the most committed team members to rise to the top and find success when faced with adversity. In times of adversity, weak members will quit, but that is understandable, as people need to have the basics of survival food and shelter, so they do not deal well with uncertainty. Having this transparency is also a great benefit when times are good. We can share in one another's successes and celebrate wins as an open and communicative team.

The second principle is leadership. I'm confident any employee in our organization would tell you that the opportunity for advancement is always present, that if you work hard enough, innovate with great ideas, and are an open, honest team player, you can go from assistant to manager to president to CEO in record time. Stepping it up in any position should yield results for both employer and employee. The employees at KICVentures who advance most quickly are the ones who say, "Leadership isn't just a title; leadership starts with me, to lead by example from out in front." Managers are often blamed for decreased productivity, and that might be deserved, but in our system, that is unacceptable because everyone should take a leadership role in their day-to-day activities. Leadership means being an example and taking ownership to get the job done. Be all in to succeed. Leadership is not just delegation and management; it is leading from the front, going out there, and working harder than everyone else, setting the pace and example.

The third principle is knowledge sharing. One of the biggest challenges I consistently pose to my management team is, "Do we actually have the knowledge to know what to do next and to analyze and solve problems? How do you think your way out of a paper bag if you don't even understand what it means to be in a paper bag or why you want to get out?" I push them to recognize that we need to stay hungry and seek knowledge to equip ourselves for success. We do this by sharing external articles, attending conferences, and doing extensive research on best practices and the competition. These articles don't just get shared by the executive team with directors and managers; we share these articles with everyone in the company (remember, communication is key). If an article or conference can inspire a junior member of the staff, if it lights a fire under them because they recognize their lack of knowledge and want to change it, it will push all of us to be better and to advance.

The fourth principle is attitude. We specifically hire for attitude, not just technical skills. I grew up a young, inexperienced but hungry kid from Jamaica. My attitude was to learn from everyone I could and strive to be better. Plain and simple, I wanted to succeed and to achieve financial stability, and I was willing to listen and be molded by anyone who cared to help me get there. I believe it's important to give the hardworking, ambitious people in this world a fair shot, regardless of their résumé, if they too want to succeed and are seeking help. If they have the right work ethic and a great attitude, they deserve the same chance as anyone else. Skills are learnable, teachable, and recordable, but attitude is an unquantifiable and important aspect of an employee. During the tough times, the long days, and the late hours, it's not skills that get us through the day; it's our attitude. Remember, skills can be improved through training, but attitude comes from within.

The fifth principle is developing processes and having metrics—to assess how well or how poorly we are doing. In order to prove success, both individually and as an organization, there must be data to back it up. Sales numbers, employee surveys, and customer satisfaction polls are just a few of the data points an organization has at its disposal. These numbers predict success, failure, challenges, and opportunities if they are watched closely by those who know where to look.

To maintain a strong culture, I focus on identifying the habits that we value at each level. We also focus on establishing processes and systems as we go, and these form the building blocks for sustaining the company as we change toward scaling up. When we hire, we want to bring new employees into a culture, not have them come in and function just on their talents or experience.

I often say, "Data doesn't lie," but data doesn't mean anything unless a team is committed to managing the data and using it to evaluate and set actionable plans. Managing sales data is Business 101, and we learned the hard way that it cannot be ignored until the end of the year or even the end of the quarter. We need day-by-day trends so we can make day-by-day adjustments, because our customers don't take kindly to bad experiences and will not wait around for them to improve. Making adjustments to a process might take months, but it's imperative that these shifts are made, and in the meantime, business will suffer.

The bottom line is that you need a working team with the right attributes to execute your vision. You need principles that everyone, especially your customers, are familiar with. We developed our principles through the process of asking ourselves how we improve employee satisfaction to get a higher TQ.

Start by recognizing what attributes you want the group to value. Be clear with them that you value the team working together above all else. Let them know that working together, you will be able to set goals and reach them, and that will build confidence. Each goal you achieve is a win, but it is not winning versus losing. Get them to start setting small, reachable goals, and after each failure or win, discuss what the team did well, what they can learn from and do better, and what adjustment they need to make. You want your team to thrive and grow together, so you want a culture in which people feel valued for their individual contributions, but their actions must put the team first. Everyone should know what the team is asking of them and what they can do for the team, then commit to doing it.

Invest in building group morale; be directly involved. I make it clear to my team that before we do anything, I expect them to focus on preparation and planning. I want them to become experts and to build their knowledge. This is where we value chalkboarding the most. I then encourage them to use that preparation and knowledge to solve problems. I provide measurable rewards when appropriate. Let them know that even after the preparation and giving it all our effort, we are not afraid to fail, so we take calculated risks. We are nimble, always learning and acting on more information. The key is we can make adjustments quickly. We want to fail fast because we are prepared to act on failures, solve problems, and innovate new approaches.

In order to scale our business, I recognize the need to establish processes and systems that the right team can own and use to be effective. We also train our team members to have cross-functional roles by keeping information transparent so that everyone knows what everyone else knows. We are constantly forming and unforming teams to drive tasks quickly and effectively. We have many products and different companies and limited cash, so our key people have to be flexible to work on new projects quickly and then move to another project just as quickly and get it to completion. Often, each team member is working on more than one team, as tasks overlap in completion times. This model of small teams changes at each level we grow to, and this may mean we are changing our team at each level or adding new members. Changing many of the team members as you level up your company is a must, as you will need more experience and competence. It is common to contract our team size and then rebuild. We are an investment firm with multiple portfolio companies, so we have the capability to hire into each company separate from our core management team that sits at KICVentures' executive level. This allows us to have a smaller team since many activities are duplicated across the different companies. By centralizing these activities, the companies can all benefit from a single action by a single member of the team. For example, we have one team that manages logistics for all the companies; no need to duplicate logistics across each company. We try to keep key team members on our management team to help train the new members and sustain the core culture, but this is difficult to do since some people grow out of the company or just hit a ceiling. To maintain a strong culture, I focus on identifying the habits that we value and keep valuing at each level. These habits become our routine, but there is nothing routine about habits, as habits are critical to how you perform daily and avoid mistakes. We also focus on establishing processes and systems as we go, and these form the building blocks for sustaining the company as we change toward scaling up. When we hire, we want to bring new employees into a culture, not have them come in and function just on their talents or experience.

Let's go back to the ground level. If you don't have a team in place, how do you start to build one to get your business off the ground? If you are lucky, you will find people who will work for a payday, not just a paycheck. People who work for a paycheck are so blinded by every penny they can make they usually only work if they can directly tie how hard they work or how much time they put in with how it affects their paycheck. This is bad for team morale. They will infect your team without having to say much, because everyone can pick them out. They will find ways to kill time rather than do real work and will always look for opportunities to make sure everyone sees what they do for the company and the team. They will remind you they could make more somewhere else. This is part of how they try to build goodwill in the bank for when they let down the team or disappear early from work or avoid working at home after hours or on a weekend. What they put in the bank will be their guilt card. They tend to be lazy as well, doing only enough to keep their jobs and never taking ownership to see projects through to the end, because they would then have to focus on a new project.

Here are some interview questions to ask your new hires to

ensure they are true team players: Ask what they really want to do with their lives and why they want to work with you and your company. I ask how their kids or someone close to them would describe them. I ask how they feel about money. These questions usually let them start talking about their personal lives, and I look for opportunities to ask follow-up questions to understand them on a deeper level. What is their attitude? You want to surround yourself with those who share your attitude toward work and other people. Are they someone you'd enjoy going out and having a drink with, meeting their families, and spending time with them? You don't want people who have an acidic attitude or who make you feel uncomfortable. Avoid fluff from people who make promises that cause you to hope they can deliver, because you need to succeed so badly you feel you can tolerate working with anyone. Ask them about their previous jobs and about specific projects they worked on to get details about their roles and how they measured themselves and the outcome. I made lots of mistakes by not speaking to prior employees. I think calling a prior employee is a great way to get some insights into a potential hire.

My first employee at our first medical device company under KICVentures took a pay cut to come work with me, so I made him an equity partner. He was a dedicated, loyal, hardworking, team-oriented person. He was a great listener, nonconfrontational, and a very even-keel guy. He never complained when we had to hire new employees and pay them more, because he wanted the company to grow and succeed more than he cared about his own feelings. He had no sense of entitlement. He cared most about our success and was invested in the idea that one day success would generate a payday, not just a paycheck, and that people could benefit from our company's success. Both of us saw our paychecks as just what we needed to live. It used to bother us a lot when we hired someone with great talent, and we invested in their training, and then they would leave for another job that had a higher salary. A payday to them was not a sure thing, and they could not predict when that day would come.

The cofounder of KICVentures, Aditya Humad, was a student of mine at the University of Pennsylvania when I met him. He went on to graduate from the Wharton Undergraduate Business Program and worked at J.P. Morgan before he decided to join up with me. He has never asked me for a raise, and he is the CFO, so he pays everyone, including new hires, who make more than his salary. Many of our team members share similar attributes; they know who they are, and I thank them for their years of loyalty. The point is these people will work the hardest to get things done because they are building a team that is working toward success and a payday. That is their reward. The ability to accept delayed gratification is a priceless trait for team members who help build success. Hire for the right attitude that fits your culture.

BRING THE RIGHT PEOPLE ON BOARD

Now you know that you want people who will form a team working toward a payday, not just a paycheck. You might ask next if there are specific types of skills you need to look for in hiring. Regardless of the business, I believe you should start with an accountant who can also do your taxes. The word *account* is part of "accountant," reminding you to account for every penny you spend or receive in the early stages of your business. Every decision you make should be done with full disclosure to your accountant, and you should be aware of the tax consequences. Many a business has failed because they ran out of funds or spent their money foolishly, or worse, they make a lot of money but do not account for their taxes and run into problems with the IRS. They may even have to file bankruptcy, or company leaders may have to serve jail time for breaking the tax laws. This latter point is why I recommend that your second hire be a lawyer. You need to decide on the best type of corporate structure, have all your legal documents properly executed, and have risk management addressed in every contract. Lawyers often get a bad rap, but for many important reasons, you will want them to be on your side before you get in trouble.

The next person you need on your team is not actually employed by your company. Get a friend, experienced family member, or a mentor you can bounce ideas off of. I used to call my sister every time I had an important business decision to make; sometimes I called her every day. She had a lot of experience working for an advertising company, where she saw the owners build it up and then fail. She warned me to keep my team small and to keep people busy before hiring new employees, because people like to feel valued. When they have a lot of work and your attention, they feel valued. She told me to keep the team working closely together, to not put people in large offices or shower them with too much money in the beginning.

If people feel you have a lot of money to spend, they will be looking for you to spend it on them, and that can destroy team unity. If you show that you are spending a lot on yourself, they will be envious and feel you should do more for them. My sister once told me about a grand party one of the owners of her company threw at his lavish home. You would think employees would be grateful and enjoy the gesture, but no, everyone left talking about how they would have preferred that he had spent the money on bonuses rather than inviting them to a party. Even with all my successes and with millions of dollars earned by our companies, I still only pay myself $50,000 per year in salary and make up the rest to cover my expenses from my practice as a surgeon. Surgery is my day job, and not taxing the company's cash is prudent. Working and contributing revenues directly from my labor keeps me feeling like one of the employees who is fulfilling my role and getting paid for it, rather than the boss or leader. So I take a draw from my practice of what I need to cover my expenses, and the rest goes back to the employees and to grow the practice. You should not throw your personal money information around, but at times, it can be effective in demonstrating that you are working to build the organization for a future large payday and that you are willing to make sacrifices for the company to succeed; in other words, you are making concessions similar to what you are asking others to make.

Train your first employee from the ground up. Select someone who is excited by the opportunity to work closely with you and who will put the business first. Attitude is key here; you want someone who respects you and is a giver, not a taker. You still must be the one to do the most work in the beginning, which saves money. But you also must limit the damage from mistakes you will be guaranteed to make. If you choose someone who knows more about the business than you do, then you should not be starting that business from the ground up. In that case, you just don't know the business well enough. If you are buying a company, that is a different story. You may risk having your business plan stolen by that person after they get frustrated working for you, because your lack of knowledge is a perceived weakness.

It's very different, however, if you pick someone who is more of an expert than you are, and you trust them to build a team around their expertise—but with your mission and vision. It is a great thing to hire people who are better than you at aspects of the business. In fact, this is what you ultimately want to achieve: growing your team by hiring top people who are better than you at what they do, so you can focus on the overall business mission.

I know it sounds counterintuitive, that it's a bad thing to hire someone who knows the business more than you do in the early stages. My advice is that if you have such a person early on, make them a consultant or your mentor; they don't have to work directly on your team to help you. I know someone whose father was one of the first employees in a company being run by the founder, which is now franchised in multiple locations and countries. The employee and the founder kept butting heads. The founder wanted to do it one way because he saw the opportunity to be different and to change the industry, but his employee knew more than he did about the business, so he kept trying to tell him how it had been done and how it should be done the right way. The founder eventually fired the employee and built a team around himself to advise him on how to execute his vision. Now he flies around on private jets and sails around on his yachts and has all the objects of a successful lifestyle. The former employee is no longer in the business and missed a great opportunity. The founder did the right thing to cut ties early enough when he was at war trying to get his company to exist. I so admired his success formula; I looked to his story early on as an example to follow. At KICVentures, you will see that we are building a symbiotic group of companies focused on health care, with a close core management team. We do this because I saw how this entrepreneur handled a similar model in his industry.

Once you have the personnel to get the business started, the next set of hires should be focused on the product. This is where you need the best experts. If you cannot get the best experts, then get employees with the right attitude, people excited to learn who will fit in with the team. Get everyone to work together to get the product to be great. I hired an industrial designer who had worked on designing instruments and devices that had made it to market. He was at a successful design firm that had a great team culture. I did not have to train him, except on our mission, values, goals, and the overall business. To bring our first product to market, we hired an outside firm to work with us on our design ideas and to get our product out the door.

This is important; if you try to do it all too early, it will cost a lot of cash, and you will waste a lot of time learning from the plethora of mistakes you will make. With an outside firm helping us, we gradually hired more people and learned from our consultants so we could eventually do it all on our own. KICVentures is now embarking on a rapid growth phase; our staff works with several outside key companies and personnel to manage our growth. This is an important lesson to show your people that you are willing to seek help and not overburden them, or worse, promote your best people into positions in which they become incompetent.

THINK OF THE PARTS OF YOUR BUSINESS AS PARTS OF THE BODY

From here, I suggest you think of your business as a living being. I think of each company as a person. Who are the brains, the heart, and the limbs? How do you put this body together? First, I build a core team that works the closest with me. They are the brains. I build a special projects team that I call our right brain. Our executive team is the frontal lobe; they make the decisions and understand the emotions of the business and the people. The left brain is comprised of product development and quality team leaders who ensure we have the technical issues around our products well covered. The customer service, training, and supply chain team leaders make up the posterior brain that keeps the company steady and balanced as we grow. From this core team that composes the brain, we build the rest of the body to get the work done, day to day. People also need to know what part of the body they are. For example, are they a hand or a brain? The hand is not the brain, so don't ask it to function as the brain, and vice versa.

Your core team, the individuals you bring on to work the closest with you, will set the foundation and tone of your company; they should have a sense of ownership. They should have your back, and you should have theirs; there should be full transparency among the parts of this brain. You can have connections, money, and the perfect business plan, but if you don't have a working team to carry out your vision, the company will fail.

Trying to discern the right people for the job can be a complicated process, so start by identifying what type of management style you possess. Are you laissez-faire, allowing the people who work for you to have the utmost autonomy? Are you participatory and need to be involved in every decision? Do you prioritize your employees' happiness or the task at hand? Identify your management style and consistently lead with authority. This will give you great insight into the type of professionals you should hire and will give those individuals confidence in your ability to lead.

It is important to choose people who not only work with your management style but thrive in it. Every person is unique and has a unique approach to their professional lives. If you hire people who do not respond well to your management style, even if they are extremely talented, you will only harm your company and limit production, because your turnover rate will be high, and these people will breed bad faith among your team before they leave. Have the foresight to look at the big picture and envision how your employees will come together to work efficiently as a team.

At KICVentures, members of my creative and engineering team are creative and nimble, and for that reason, I love to devote much of my time to working closely with them to ensure we stay on course and follow the company's vision, mission, and purpose. I seek people who are youthful creatives: writers, designers, branding and marketing specialists, thinkers, and innovators. When brainstorming on branding, I ask, "If you removed our name from the message, would you know it is our company?" If the answer is no, then we make the changes so that we are identifiable even without our logo. I involve my leadership team to incubate new ideas, at times turning these ideas into companies. Any new company we bring into our portfolio gets vetted to ensure it is aligned with our mission, values, and goals. We then look to hire a strong president and chief operating officer (COO) to run this new company, or we promote someone from within or simply share management among our leadership management team.

Your sales department should be the feet of your company,

spreading the product messages throughout all marketing and social networking platforms. The branding and creative department fulfills the role of the company's voice, guaranteeing that our message is accurately heard and received by our target segment audience.

> Your core team, the individuals you bring on to work
> the closest with you, will set the foundation and tone
> of your company and have a sense of ownership.

Supervisors and managers act as the eyes and ears, ensuring work is done with quality and precision, determined by the brain. Many of our departments act as the muscles, arms, and hands of the company, ensuring work is done effectively and efficiently. These divisions put their time and energy into creating tangible products and transforming the company's vision into a reality.

No part of the body is more or less important than another within the company. For this reason, it is important to treat all employees with value and care, understanding that they play a vital role in achieving the company's success. How will the brain achieve its plan without the hands to make it happen? How will the heart's mission be fulfilled without the voice and feet to bring it to the public? Every role is important, and as the leader of the company, it is your job to recognize this and make the body work together as a team.

As it says in the Bible, "The eye cannot say to the hand, 'I don't need you!' And the head cannot say to the feet, 'I don't need you!' On the contrary, those parts of the body that seem to be weaker are indispensable, and the parts that we think are less honorable we treat with special honor" (1 Corinthians 12:21–23).

No one is disposable, especially after you have invested in training them, emotionally and financially. However, you need committed, competent winners to build a working team that will ultimately win you success. Anybody who does not demonstrate that they are a committed team member you must part ways with as soon as possible. Think of your business as we do a human body, and you will ensure that your company is healthy and thriving, hopefully taken care of as well as (or better than) you as the leader take care of your own body. Get all the parts working together, and you can take on any goal and achieve it. If you do not have a working team, you will have limited potential in the business industry, even if you believe you have a talented group of winners.

What are the most important qualities you look for in team members? Share with us.

QUICK RECAP

Lessons on Team Building:

1. Hire talented winners to build a working team, and they will find ways to win.
2. Approach all tasks by forming and unforming teams. No one person can do it better or faster than the collective team.
3. Prepare your team to manage success and failure.
4. Set achievable goals for your team. Small successes prepare them for larger tasks.
5. Find team players who value a payday over a paycheck and create a core management team.
6. Know what makes your team members tick. Ask what they want for themselves.
7. Make the same financial concessions you ask others to make.
8. Embrace training your employees from the ground up, and hire people with a learning attitude.
9. Your company functions as one, but design your teams like parts of a body. Optimize their strengths and functions.
10. Know your management style but be willing to learn, and choose people who thrive with it.

CHAPTER 4
ESSENTIAL KEY #4
SCHEDULE CHALKBOARDING
SESSIONS TO GET THE BEST OUT
OF AN IDEA AND YOUR TEAM

Chalkboarding with your team puts everyone in an equal
position, wherein they don't need to be right, just involved.

I have come to believe that the most important leadership tool is
scheduling your time in functional blocks. Determine a task and
clock time to focus on that task. I used to make a to-do list for the
day, but I found it guilted me into feeling like I was failing at my list,
versus when I blocked time and formed a team to complete a task in
that time. If we have to go over, we make adjustments for the day, but
the goal is to finish the task that we attack, not complete the to-do
list. It is important to recognize that as leaders succeed, their time
grows increasingly limited. You must therefore find ways to become
more efficient, optimize your time (and help people manage their
time), and use tools and processes more effectively. Start by ensuring
you have the most knowledge about what you are going to do and
then develop your plans and strategies so you can prepare to successfully complete all your initiatives. Next, schedule all your activities

so your time is constrained by your schedule and is therefore less likely to be wasted on unscheduled activities.

In our planning, our team has found scheduling chalkboarding sessions to be an effective and efficient tool for project management. This chapter will describe this tool, and I recommend you use it in every meeting, big or small, to ensure you thoroughly explore all options, write down the action plan, and delineate who is responsible for each action. Chalkboarding does not have to be literal, as today we have online and digital collaborative software tools that allow even remote collaboration without anyone writing on a chalkboard fixated to a wall in an office. A promise to do something is only as good as the paper it is written on and the person who's going to be held accountable for doing it. Too often, you find people who say they are "working on it" or that they understand what you are asking, but you find out later this was not true. Often when people say they are working on something, it really means they have not fully explored what needs to be done and will just figure it out.

Chalkboarding is having your team (including you) stand around a whiteboard or online and brainstorm together, using tools like colored eraser pens, writing down and erasing ideas as they come to you, and then delegating actionable items to individuals with timelines for completion. All this sounds like traditional chalkboarding, but it can be done digitally today; the idea is the same. We always start with the problem, the goals, and the resources because these three topics generally represent what you would consider when starting on a journey, and every idea or project is like a journey. Other categories come up along the way.

When you chalkboard, you overcome procrastination, as if the entire team is saying, "Let's solve this now." It forces a sense of urgency and requires everyone to pool their time into one block, so you magnify that productivity. Everyone shares their knowledge, so you don't have one person who knows everything. Chalkboarding is about love and focus—love for what you do and the people you want to do it with, plus the collective focus that will drive your team to succeed.

As the leader, if you feel you have a magic potion to make the company successful, then you must drink the potion for everyone to see, not expect everyone else to drink the potion without you demonstrating the ultimate confidence of drinking it yourself. Furthermore, the people who drink the potion should help you make it, so they also believe in it. Chalkboarding is like you making a potion with your team and together drinking it with the group.

Chalkboarding with your team puts everyone in an equal position, wherein they don't need to be right, just involved. It enables everyone on your team to brainstorm about a particular topic, to throw things out and think freely without fear of ridicule. It levels the company horizontally; everyone knows what everyone else is expected to do and when. After the session is over, ensure that this knowledge is shared with everyone via email.

NO GOING IT ALONE

We have a rule in our companies that states no one should work on a project alone, no matter how small the task. When people work by themselves, they usually fail or get subpar results, while a team offers more checks and balances by having more people involved. Approach each activity like a project, form the team with a team leader who takes ownership of the goals, and add as many people as you need so the project can be done effectively and as quickly as possible. We then chalkboard with that team, and I make sure that, as the CEO, I am involved. What do I add? My presence is a positive force, and team members can get my attention, so I can learn more about them. I help keep everyone focused on the big business picture and help keep a framework so we don't wander off course. It is also a great teaching opportunity for all of us, if a teachable topic comes up. This is one of our habits. We expect people to quickly form and unform teams as they go from goal to goal. This means you leverage competences from different people rather than grow the overall employee pool just to have people joining to fill a single competency. We value a culture where people are eager to learn and apply what they have learn, so they grow instead of just doing what they know over and over again, confined to a single job.

An important aspect of chalkboarding is that the leader must be prepared and know more than everyone else about the business impact of the ideas the group generates; otherwise, the leader might make decisions without the appropriate knowledge and, worse, might frustrate members of the group who are better prepared but who look to the leader to make decisions. In cases where no one else is really prepared, it is like the blind leading the blind.

Leaders must therefore be prepared and fully engaged in every session; they must be decisive. I cannot think of a worse outcome than the leader not fully understanding the issues, sanctioning a bad plan, and sending the team off to go work on it. Whenever I've empowered one individual to manage a project without a team chalkboarding, the person has failed, and many times, they ended up quitting the company later, as they became frustrated by poor results or having to change course.

Some employees exhibit a lot of confidence because they feel they're an island or a one-man army; it's all or nothing for them. It's their way or the highway. Their confidence is a disguise for what they are thinking, which is, *I want to do things my way and on my timeline, so don't worry. I got this. Just wait and see.* This is a big problem because things change fast while they are in their cocoon, and you don't know the exact details of their planning or how to factor them into your changing plans. So while they're thinking of winning big, you and the company could lose big, and time lost cannot be bought back. They will also set their own schedule, and when you approach them, they will always say they are working on it.

The other problem with having one person fully empowered on a project is that it's not as fun or fulfilling for that person or the team as it is when the team chalkboards a new idea and everyone has a defined role and sense of dependence. To really appreciate chalkboarding, do it for yourself on your own projects. I do this on my phone, taking notes while I plan for my personal goals and those of the companies I run. I do the research online and formulate, write down, and commit to my ideas and strategies before I engage the company. If you fail to plan and write those plans down, you are planning to fail.

When your individual team members constantly come back and share the chalkboarding activity, the bond within the team will strengthen, as will their connection to the company culture and vision. There is strength in numbers through chalkboarding. While doing this, we think in terms of team first.

How do you communicate with your team? Share with us..

QUICK RECAP

Lessons on Chalkboarding:

1. Chalkboard every task before starting.
2. Chalkboarding breaks down tasks into tangible steps.
3. Chalkboarding makes it clear who is responsible for each step.
4. Through chalkboarding, you say, "This is urgent. Let's get it done."
5. Chalkboarding magnifies individual and collective productivity.
6. Lead a chalkboarding session by keeping people focused on the business's big picture.
7. Chalkboarding naturally strengthens a team's bond.

8. Chalkboarding puts everyone in an equal position and allows them to think freely.
9. Chalkboarding brings out the characteristics of each employee.
10. Passionate individuals can spread their enthusiasm to the team through chalkboarding sessions.

CHAPTER 5
ESSENTIAL KEY #5

WORK HARD AND BE HANDS-ON

In moments of need, stick your hands out
and use them to help yourself.

B e aware: I am going to spend lots of time on this chapter, and if you follow the lessons in just this chapter, you might have enough to be successful. A patient of mine once asked me who I would turn to if I needed help with my businesses. I hesitated and started to think of all the people I could call on in an emergency. I hoped it was a trick question, because I did not know anyone I could count on 100 percent to help me in a business emergency. This made me anxious, so I gave up and asked why he asked the question. He took both of my hands, held them out in front of me with my palms up, and asked me again. I was now even more perplexed, so he gave me the answer: "In moments of need, stick your hands out and use them to help yourself."

KEEP YOUR DAY JOB

To achieve any goal, prepare to work hard for it and get your hands dirty. Avoid the strong temptation of looking for a quick success or finding someone to do it for you; don't sit around your corner office, worrying about all the things that could go wrong. It amazes me how each time I hear someone come up with a new idea to do something, I hear someone else mention how much work it will take, or how much money it will cost, or how things could go wrong, or how it is not that simple. In starting a business, like pursuing any goal, you need a positive attitude to succeed. You must prepare yourself mentally to work hard and be hands-on, to make enough money to pay your bills and keep your business alive. No one succeeds at anything without working hard at it day in and day out and over time falling and rising, failing and making mistakes, again and again. Working hard and persevering are two absolutely necessary traits to succeed. If it took work and risks to breathe every day, many people would die from laziness and fear of taking a risk—until they were on their deathbed, realizing they were about to die. For many people who are just comfortable with their lives, they have died in spirit, but they still have time on the clock before their physical death.

So you have decided to be brave and start your own venture. How do you survive? is the first question to ask. In the beginning of starting a new venture, you are fighting to stay alive and to exist. It is about surviving. There is no time to be glamorous. Just put your head down and focus on the day-to-day activities to keep you going forward. Your greatest risk is to run out of money. This is one of the reasons to keep a day job until your business is self-sustainable. Word of caution here. If you slack off on your day job, you are robbing the company you work for and yourself, since excellence is a character trait that you don't turn on and off. Also, karma can be real. If you slack off on your job, you will likely carry that experience with you, so there is always that feeling that you know how to slack off. Hardworking people don't develop the experience to slack off, so they are always looking to work hard, even when it is not their company. It might be that time is really what you need in order to succeed, so spending time on your venture means you will likely not need as much money. Plus, if you dedicate time, you will likely build value, which attracts money. If you can work full-time on your company, then you make up for lack of money or other resources with your hard labor. Working smart is desired, but in the early stages of starting or leading a company, you need to just put your head down and work long, hard hours consistently. This is the time you work late at night and get up bright and early, with passion to do it again the next day. Each day brings new hope and problems to solve. When you study highly successful entrepreneurs, it is usual to hear they work a hundred hours per week, and they sleep no more than six hours, so they have eighteen hours in each day to balance work, family, and recreation, with little wasted time.

Later in the book, we talk about why there is really no place for pride in business, especially in the start-up phase. Working hard and being hands-on is what it takes to keep your business alive. As you grow the company, your experience and confidence will also grow, and you can put greater emphasis on working smarter and more effectively. This doesn't mean looking for shortcuts but rather being more strategic. This is called the heads-up phase of your business. But the beginning of your business is the heads-down phase. I used to question the real benefits of my college years until I started my own business and realized the importance of the training we went through of receiving a homework assignment and a deadline, doing this week after week until graduation. College was as much about gaining the knowledge about daily habits of filing up your calendar with scheduled activities as it was about gaining hard knowledge. Results follow deliberate activities; so do consequences. If you miss deadlines, do not show up to classes, and do crappy work, you get a crappy grade. If you are disciplined and do great work, you get a great grade. If you miss the deadline, you get a zero grade. If you must stay up all night, that is your choice. Maybe we should make all tasks in our business like a homework assignment in college.

There is something to be said for keeping a regular job throughout the process of developing your business. For one, it forces you to work more hours in the day (that you would probably otherwise waste), and you will learn to be efficient with your time. I would assume that before you started your company or were promoted to CEO, you learned how to be a great employee and how to be managed. If you are not someone who can be managed and you hate having a boss, you would be well served to take the time to transform yourself into a great employee and team player while working for someone else, before jumping full-time into leading people. Think about a person who joined the armed services who started out in boot camp but later rose to become a general. I would expect a great general to have been a great soldier. I imagine the best college professors were also great students; otherwise, why would anyone want to follow a general who has lousy habits or learn from a professor who does not encourage you to be a great student?

When you employ others, you are likely to be the type of boss you were when you worked for someone else. I see employees who don't take ownership of their work, so they kill time sitting at their desk. As soon as they leave work, they completely turn off and don't care about what happens to the project. They do not want to be accessible to anyone at work. Very frustrating if you are trying to succeed, but you feel there are people around you who don't care about succeeding; it is more about keeping their job and being comfortable. Imagine if you are working hard to complete a project and you need help from someone on the team, but they refuse to answer your call when they know it is you who is calling. It can kill your desire and build resentment. These same employees are difficult and feel that starting their own business is their goal because they hate to work for any boss and do not want to feel obligated to anyone else on the team. They will find that these same traits will doom their success because when you are the boss, you have to own the projects; there are no days off, and if you're not paying attention to the project, you can't make sure it succeeds. A real boss works as long as is needed and is always available twenty-four seven because they know that the potential to help someone solve a problem and foster teamwork is in a single phone call. Bottom line, if you are a terrible soldier, you will be a terrible boss or leader. I make it a habit to work on all my projects every day, including holidays and vacation, unless there is just no time, like when I am with family. If I don't take your call right away, I will return your call as soon as possible, usually within minutes. My personal life is enriched when my business life is going well, and my business life is enriched when my personal life is going well. This is the life of a boss, but I was always doing as much as I could with my time and sleeping less than eight hours a night as a soldier before I became a boss.

A good exercise to help you focus on becoming a great employee is to write your own executive summary, as you would if you were starting a business. Start by writing about the background of the business from your understanding of it, and then write your mission for the business. What will you do for the business to succeed? Add a vision statement to paint a picture of where you see yourself eventually when you do succeed. Next, what are the problems facing the company, and how can you personally solve them? List solutions for these problems and the opportunities for you when you solve them. Lastly, what are the tasks and goals, the ones and zeros, the basic tasks you need to accomplish—and on what timeline? You can show this summary to your managers and human resources supervisors and see if they agree with it. Then focus on staying on track by using your summary as a tool, a guide, and a daily record of how effectively you are accomplishing your goals. If you do this, you will rise up the ladder within your company, as this shows you are organized to succeed for the company.

This may sound like a lot of work, and I expect you are reading this book not for me to give you homework to do. However, this is exactly my point; you will need to sit down and write an executive summary to start your venture or risk failing quickly. In addition, you will need to work hard, pay attention to details, and be organized, even more so when you start your own business. If you are an employee, try to view your job as an opportunity to learn from the bottom up about how businesses operate. Learn from the experience and take whatever lessons from it you can. In life and in general, you get out what you put in.

Why should you be a great employee? This is like asking why you should be considerate or nice. We should approach every job to do our best to learn and grow and be a team player. There are lots of rewards when you apply yourself to do things well and get results. Maybe your boss could be your mentor and future investor. Maybe you need a reference, or you want to make a higher salary. Allow the job to give you humility and teach you how to take direction, build teams, complete projects, be reliable, do great work, build consistency, develop your patience, and network. If it's a job you hate, understand why and take that feeling with you to the next job or to your start-up, to remind you of how bad it felt working for the wrong person or company. Or maybe you were the problem, and you can try to fix it. The effort you put into your current job can produce results beyond your expectations, if you are willing to invest time in accomplishing your own goals within your job. Take from the opportunity everything you possibly can, while also financially supporting your personal business endeavors.

> Your employees should sense that there is no job you will ask them to do that you are not willing to do yourself.

Someday, when you sit at the top of your own firm, or if you are sitting at the tip of any firm, you should remember what it was like to be an employee, and this will hopefully spur you to be hands-on in helping those you lead to enjoy working with you and to feel they are growing and achieving success like you did. To be a successful boss, you must be viewed as someone who listens to the concerns of others and is empathetic and caring about their personal satisfaction. Show self-discipline and reward discipline. This will inspire employees to follow your lead (maybe because it's apparent you remember what it was like to be an employee, and you are still working side by side with the team, owning your role, not just delegating). You want to earn your employees' respect, and ways to do that include leading by example, being responsive to what they are experiencing, and creating a culture where everyone feels appreciated. Your employees should sense that there is no job you will ask them to do that you are not willing to do yourself. They should feel they are working toward goals and a vision they see themselves benefitting from and they feel is worth their commitment.

I find that I get better results if I start doing a part of the job that I ask someone else to do, because it helps clarify what I want them to do. Most of the time, I have more clarity about the end results and the why than they do, so it saves time when I help out at the beginning and don't just delegate the entire project. This also helps build a sense of ownership and trust. Delegation often slows down results, and the outcome is usually not exactly what you want, but it is necessary to allow employees to feel appreciated and that they are learning. I recently began to write a brief executive summary of any job I was asking someone else to do, so they were clear on the reasons and expectations for the job. I also bring in early all the people who will need to know about the project, plus those who will likely form the team. This way, we are all clear before we start. I have extended this strategy to ask new employees joining us to define how they view the job and what they want to accomplish and in what timeframe. There should be no ambiguity on your expectations and the employee's expectations.

Even though I am the CEO of the multiple health-tech port-folio companies below KICVentures Group, I am still a practicing surgeon seeing patients. I run businesses across the globe, but I still make time to see patients each week in my multiple offices. With improvements in video conferencing applications, I can use tele-health to see patients without having to travel. Why do I do this? Because it keeps me working hard as a habit, keeps me hands-on with my business, keeps me in touch with my patients (who are my customers), and keeps me close to the employees who keep my companies alive and growing. Being hands-on gives me perspective. It keeps me fresh. It enables me to speak face-to-face with people who can give me invaluable insights into the success of my ventures, what direction we need take, and potential failures. It also keeps me humble, constantly reminding me that everything I am doing will affect whether I still have customers who want to walk through the door to see me for their care. My customers are my teachers. I learn from them, and they grade me.

As I build success, it further motivates me to work harder, do better, and provide even more innovations within the health care industry for my customers and employees. It is vital to be hands-on with the people around you, because without direct, physical invest-ment in the work of a company, you miss valuable opportunities for innovation, creativity, and improving the system. Work hard and dedicate time to the people around you, whether you are the lowest or highest in status.

LEAD BY EXAMPLE, LEAD OUT FRONT

You made it. You are now the boss of the company or your own company. Do you now feel you're above getting your hands involved in the day-to-day work, and there should be no reason for you to have to work hard because you're the leader? Not so fast. It may seem obvious, but one of the biggest roadblocks on the path to success is failing to work hard consistently. I have not met anyone who got fired from a job, or whose company failed, who said they didn't work hard. But did they *really* work hard, or just not hard enough, or only in spurts when the feeling moved them, or on their own terms and timeline? I know what it feels like to have that burning passion inside of you, to have the desire to do great things and achieve your goals. But if that desire is not prioritized and acted upon with consistent hard work, the desire will never amount to anything more than a dream or wasted effort and time, yours and everyone who followed you. Dreaming is good, but you also need to be grounded in reality and ready to work as hard as possible for what you want. Your drive to get things done will inspire hope that you will succeed. Drive is an attitude of strength and is an essential ingredient for leadership. People will believe in you and follow you and join in your labor, more so than just work for you while you sit, watch, and give orders.

> Drive is an attitude of strength and is an essential ingredient for leadership. People will believe in you and follow you and join in your labor.

As a beginning entrepreneur or when I became CEO, I was prepared to fill a lot of roles within our company early on. So make sure you act as the chief operating officer to be hands-on with every detail of the operation when you are in leadership of a new company. Only when your company gets larger do you need someone for this role other than yourself. For example, as we gained more employees and managers, I once hired a consultant, who was an experienced and intelligent person, to be our chief people officer to ensure hands-on mentorship of our managers with their teams. This was a temporary strategy to stimulate our teams to develop habits of planning and following through with their daily plans.

In the beginning, you'll need to be a hands-on people person, a mentor, and a coach. You are responsible for guiding the company in the direction that's best for the whole organization. You are the one who must check every decision last to ensure that everything is in place, before setting the ship's direction or signing off on any major decision. When called upon, you must make decisions, so know your business inside and out. Putting things off is making a decision to do nothing now. You are the visionary, but you need to get your hands into every part of the company. Start by focusing on the product or service you are selling because without the product or service, there is no customer and therefore no company. The purpose of a company is to innovate and create customers—that simple, says Petr Drucker, who is considered the father of business management. Next is to make sure the company functions, so be the salesperson, marketing leader, project manager, troubleshooter, and customer service representative as well as the CEO, so you can grow the company and at the same time gain the knowledge to make decisions confidently with time.

You, as the founder of your firm, need to fill or share all of these roles while still maintaining the vision and direction of the company. If you have people around you who also believe in your mission, or if you have the capital to immediately hire employees, some of this load can be shared with others over time. But do not expect anyone else to have the same burning desire that you do until they have real ownership as your partner.

If I am always eager to directly invest in the work of my employees, it shows them I am directly invested in the vision.

If I am always eager to directly invest in the work of my employees, it shows them I am directly invested in the vision. What's more—and I repeat—if you spend time among your employees, you might be viewed as accessible and approachable, and they will open up to you about their concerns, which puts you in a position to make meaningful and effective changes. In the early years of SpineFrontier, our first portfolio company, every morning, the entire team gathered together for thirty minutes and individually read a to-do list of key things they would work on that day and what had been completed the day prior. I would listen in by conference call if I wasn't in Boston. This ritual was important to build a culture that says, "I want to be hands-on, and we are a disciplined team." Today, I have a daily call only with the executive team from 8:15 to 9:00 a.m. eastern time, which helps with clarity of strategies, accountability, teamwork, inspiration, learning, and scaling with discipline. We have a company-wide call on Wednesday from 8:30 to 9:00 a.m. eastern time so everyone can be updated about the company and breed a sense of team spirit.

You've probably heard of the open-door policy, which enables employees to come in whenever they have something important to say. I challenge you to take it one step further: don't have an office. I didn't have an office in any of my companies for many years early on, and even now, my office is used by my team leaders as needed when I am not there. When I didn't have an office, I used the conference rooms or other spaces to touch down and do work, but most of the time, I am on the move inside and outside the company, instead of sitting behind a desk. I stop by my employees' desks to discuss how they're doing and to help with anything I can. This means when I'm in the office, anyone can get a visit from me at any time, but they know our interaction will include collaboration, not micromanagement. I love sitting in the conference room with a glass wall so employees can see me when they walk by and can drop in at any time if I am not on the phone. When I am in the office, I am there for the team, so I prioritize them. I get my work done in the office, at home, on the plane, in hotels, et cetera, since I am always trying to maximize my time to avoid waste and to be productive.

As the CEO, you are totally within your right to sit behind a big, expensive desk in the corner office. You've earned it, and the symbolism can send the message that you are the boss. But in doing so, you risk separating yourself from the employees, those important, key individuals who've made your success possible and upon whom you depend for future successes. So I urge you, if you do have the corner office and the big desk, arrange your office in an inviting way and get out from behind the desk routinely to work with people as often as possible.

In my current office, the walls are glass, and I keep my door open. I love to sit next to employees working on an important project as I hear their suggestions and concerns. I seek the thoughts of the newest recruits. Know the names of the janitorial staff members and speak with them about the company mission and vision. You have no idea who will have the next big idea; don't gamble on the hope that someone will have the courage to approach you when they have a great idea. They might not come to you unless they've already developed the habit.

OPPORTUNITIES DON'T TAKE HOLIDAYS

If you desire to develop a multimillion-dollar brand and want to do so without consistent hard work, welcome to the club of dreamers who never wake up. This club is packed, filled with people unwilling to prioritize work in their lifestyle, who therefore never achieve business success. Be prepared to work for your dream and to share your vision with confidence, knowing that your hard work will provide a foundation that will make your business unstoppable. Many people have dreams, but few are willing to prioritize their work consistently, day in and day out. Stand out among your competition, roll up your sleeves, prioritize your goals, and make sacrifices to achieve them faster. Work should be fun, after all. Life happens whether you are working or sitting at home on the couch, so make your time count. Build a legacy and financial freedom for you and your family.

> Once you have financial freedom, you can make
> every day your own personal holiday.

If you are passionate about your success, then holidays and weekends should not be an excuse to turn off. You don't control when there are government holidays that are meant to be no-work days, but you can control whether or not you work. When you have success, every day can be a holiday, so are you willing to invest today so that you are free to take holidays whenever? I treat Monday to Friday the same and let current work requirements dictate how much time I dedicate each day. My goal is to sleep four to six hours so I have eighteen to twenty hours to use. Arnold Schwarzenegger talked about this plan for his day and gave an answer to anyone who insists on sleeping at least eight hours when he said to sleep only six hours but sleep faster. Hope this made you laugh, as it did for me. What I work on and how much time I spend is based on priorities and whomever I am working with. If I am working with a go-getter who works every day, I work every day and as long as they are willing to work that day. During my weekends, I make sure I put in some work to balance the leisure time for myself and with my family. If you completely shut off every weekend, there will be times when Mondays are miserable because you are trying to catch up or find yourself confronted with new problems that you're unprepared to deal with. I find this to be more so now that social media is active all weekend, and you get to see content over the weekend that could affect your business decisions. If you are only learning of the news on Monday, that great feeling you had about the weekend will disappear so fast it will seem like it never happened.

If you do some work over the weekend and keep up with the news, say on LinkedIn, you'll feel a nice work-life balance and enter Monday feeling more prepared to continue what you've been working on and take on any surprises that await you. On holidays and weekends, I prioritize time for my family, but my business is also a priority. These are days to get a jump on your competition, who likely takes these days off. Once you have financial freedom, you can make every day your own personal holiday.

The hard work you sow throughout your entrepreneurial journey will later let you reap benefits that will surpass your competition and provide you with the lifestyle of success. When I was completing my training in orthopedic surgery at Harvard Medical School, I realized that the four years to get my medical degree (and another six years to complete my residency training) were too much time out of my life for me to just be in this state of a bubble working on becoming a doctor. I started to search for opportunities to build my business experience at the same time I was training. While I looked for an apartment to rent, I noted that the real estate market in Boston was priced way lower than in New York City. I thought that didn't make sense, so I did some research and determined that rent control had kept prices artificially low in Boston, especially in Cambridge.

I decided to invest in real estate. At the time, I had $2,000 in the bank, and I borrowed $3,000 from my mother, who had to work a second job to get the extra money to lend me, after I explained why I needed the help. My wife had another $2,000 in her savings, and we borrowed $5,000 from a friend of hers to sit in the bank as collateral. We promised her not to spend the money. I then spent every day at the bank, working with the loan officer to qualify and get a loan. I was determined to find a way.

We finally bought a two-bedroom condominium in Cambridge from a developer who was having trouble selling the units he had just renovated. Once we moved in, I immediately started to renovate, doing the work myself at nights and on weekends. In six months, I had done enough work to upgrade the unit substantially. We put the condominium on the market, sold it, and made a $100,000 profit. We then immediately bought a three-family house on Western Avenue for $300,000 with 10 percent down. We moved in, lived on the top floor, and rented out the first and second floors.

In three months, we bought a second three-family house in Cambridgeport for $500,000 and moved there, putting down 10 percent. We did another renovation while we lived on the first floor and renovated the top floor at Western Avenue, before selling it later for a huge profit. The money from these real estate deals allowed us to hire our own crew and keep buying, renovating, and selling condos to build our net worth to several million dollars before I finished medical school and residency. Every morning in the winter after it snowed, I would shovel the snow myself before going to the hospital to complete my patient rounds as a resident doctor.

Weekends and holidays were great for us, because we had more time to work on our business. While the other residents were sleeping, and on weekends when they chilled out, I put extra hours into my real estate business. If we had a week's vacation, before we went off on a trip, we made sure we put in meaningful work for a few days to catch up on outstanding issues. This is how we balanced the week with work and play. By the time I left Harvard, we had over $5 million in real estate, a condo at the Ritz Carlton in Key Biscayne, Florida, and another vacation property in Ocho Rios, Jamaica, plus positive cash flow.

While I was training at Massachusetts General Hospital, a financial planner came to speak with us residents about saving our money for retirement. I raised my hand and asked him, "What about investing in rental properties?" He was annoyed by my question, and the other residents looked at me strangely. He replied that, as surgeons in training, we would not have the time to develop properties and manage them, so it was not a good idea. "Better to invest your money in a diversified mutual fund and other retirement vehicles," he said.

I kept my pride in check and made him none the wiser. I realized he wanted us all to fit into his box, so this was a teaching moment for me—to learn to beware of opinions from so-called experts, speaking from within the protective walls of other people's companies, projecting their own ideas about their capabilities.

I learned from those real estate successes and the financial rewards, so today I maintain a consistent work ethic to set small goals and achieve them, blending each day to be no different from the next, and working consistently hard, whether it is for business, family, or play. If I turn off my work ethic, I feel lazy and risk doing a mediocre job, missing opportunities, or aiming to please those around me to fit into a certain lifestyle. Or worse: things pile up, and I have to work harder just to catch up or correct things that go wrong because of my inattention.

People who integrate work into their daily life flow and who work the hardest to get things done, rather than let things pile up on them, have the most fun. They enjoy everything they do because working hard becomes a habit and builds attentiveness to details, and they carry that over to all aspects of their lives. These are people I consistently hear say they want to succeed. They know their hard work will pay off one day; they will have the financial freedom to relax when they want to on their own terms.

DON'T TRADE TIME AND HEALTH FOR WEALTH

Working hard always has rewards, but if you are trading your time and your health for money, you should use this book to change your approach. Understand how you spend your time working hard before you just forge ahead and start working long hours because you think that will guarantee success. The key is to achieve a work-life balance, which is easier said than done. So first, decide whether your strength is in using your brain to come up with strategies and formulating the steps to execute those strategies, or if it is better for the company if you close out as many tasks as possible and leave the strategizing to others. If you spend hours working hard on the things that eat up your time, neglecting the things you really should be working on (and that give you the highest impact), then you're working hard on the wrong things. You're really losing time. So try not to just be busy (and busy on the wrong things) when you should be focused on the right priorities. I see frustrated employees who are working as hard as possible and are spread thin, but when I take a deeper look at what they're doing, I realize they're not prioritizing the important things; they're constantly busy on a lot of tasks at the same time, which is just burdensome.

> In today's business environment, networking
> and pooling your resources is a faster way to
> success and will save you a lot of time.

People feel they should spend their day being busy, but they never really finish anything. This kills time but does not bring satisfaction or growth. This reminds me of the plane that crashed while the two pilots were discussing a light that was on. As they were trying to figure out the light, they weren't paying attention to flying the plane, which is what everyone needed them to do. If you don't pay attention to what's most important and close out on them, you too might crash.

Our business empire is growing because I focus on long-term, stable investments instead of get-rich-quick schemes or ideas that require too much of my time for little return. I think of my decisions in how the results will be ten years from now, or how my life will be affected ten years from now. My strength is coming up with invest-ment strategies to deploy the cash that I worked for and managing the businesses that deploy the cash. I don't just work hard to make cash to spend on my lifestyle. Because I deployed the cash into my businesses, we now have a diversified portfolio with great cash flow and companies that will mature into major cash cows over time. My time was best spent establishing companies and systems to allow my money to work for me and buy me time from other people giving their time and getting paid to work in my businesses. This means I can accomplish many more things than if I were working alone. When you've worked hard and invested the money and time to build companies that are now working well with dependable people, you will have more time to take on more goals for the company to grow, and you will have more time to care for your health and lifestyle.

In today's business environment, networking and pooling your resources is a faster way to success and will save you a lot of time. With a smaller team, we look outside for more consultants who have the competency and who we can hold accountable to performance metrics, which is more of a challenge with employees. In fact, I think it is one of the few ways to mathematically gain time. If other people are doing work for you that you benefit from, you are gaining their time. Look around and learn from people who trade time and health for wealth, and note that they start trading other things for wealth as well, such as family, friends, and spirituality. They are working so hard to make money that it becomes their master. To avoid being sucked into this vortex, I put my health as a priority. Who doesn't like to look great and be in shape? When you are in control and wealth is not your master, you will know to make time for health. The mirror will tell you, and you will listen, but only if you make time. Otherwise, you don't even want to look. I find that if I prioritize my health, I have to manage my time, and to manage my time, I need to look at how I go about my business.

Once you are trying to conserve time, you will realize you must make friends, seek help, and look to make deals so you're not a one-person army fighting on multiple fronts. A one-person army only needs one well-placed bullet to die. That bullet could be from a health problem like a heart attack or from an external bullet to your business, like a lawsuit, an investigation of some sort, or just one bad business move. And trust me, you will make bad business moves, so be prepared.

ALL IN

So you've kept your day job, and you are leading your company by example while working to fulfill different roles in your company. Your habit of an open-door policy gives you direct involvement with your employees. You're prioritizing your business while making sure to take care of your health. How do you juggle it all? This is a legitimate question. I'm often asked how I juggle my job as a spine surgeon with running companies and making meaningful time for my family and myself. Well, I've developed a helpful mindset to make sure I juggle all the balls in the air well: the practice of being all in. Being all in is a mindset and an attitude. It means that in everything I do, big or small, I am all in. All in means focusing 100 percent on anything I decide to give my time to; otherwise, I don't do it because I know the results will end up being mediocre.

> Your day-to-day life is filled with opportunities
> to hone your street smarts.

It does not matter if it's speaking with someone for just a few seconds, reading a book to my child, or working on one of my companies, each activity gets my full focus in that moment, and if it requires more time than I have, I spend time on my own, continuing to ensure I stay fully engaged until whatever I'm trying to accomplish gets across the finish line as quickly and as well as possible. I credit this approach of being all in with my ability to finish this book by using every spare moment I had until it was completed.

STREET SMARTS

Working hard and being hands-on will get you far, but there's a third element that's crucial to the recipe for success: street smarts. You might think having a business degree would give you the smarts to succeed. Graduating with a degree in business will give you exposure to business principles and strategies, which are good tools to have, but you get street smarts from experience, and this is invaluable. What are street smarts? I think they're the gut feelings you have when you are doing business. I think you get these gut feelings because your brain is instinctively processing experience and sending you the signal. Street smarts allow you to break down the business into its simplest terms to understand how to make the right decisions seem simple and obvious.

I often sit and listen to a detailed presentation of an idea with impressive slides and figures, but they often miss two basic but very important questions: (1) how do we make money? and (2) how do we lose money? These are two questions that the person on the street, so to speak, would understand. Street smarts are acquired from real-life experiences; knowledge comes from knowing the results of your past decisions and understanding how your similar decisions will likely turn out the next time around. It is learning which chosen path led to success, which did not, and why.

This is our KISS principle: keep it simple and sensible.

Your day-to-day life is filled with opportunities to hone your street smarts. You can learn a lot about negotiating by trying to buy something from a street vendor. You can learn a lot about human nature by figuring out how people cheat or simply get around a system. Read books or watch documentaries about businesses to learn from other people's street smarts. As you interact with people and hustle to find ways to get ahead, you are cultivating street smarts. I've seen people risk their lives to attach their cable wires to another house to get electricity for free. I've also heard about people splitting the signal from their cable box in order to pay less. These street smarts made me realize the lengths certain people will go to while trying to save a buck. I used the insight from these experiences to look at ways to prevent people from cheating us out of sales.

Security systems are a valuable exercise in applying street smarts, because as cynical as it may be, I've learned through my street smarts that people will always innovate and find new ways to break your system. The solution is to break down your own systems to find points of weakness, and then you'll be able to build stronger systems and safeguards. Similarly, to understand how to best apply street smarts to succeed, break down your business to its simplest form and apply strategies to grow, while maintaining the simple core business. This is our KISS principle: keep it simple and sensible.

So be motivated to prioritize your time and health as you consistently work smart and hard in ways that most people would never choose. Build your business and network quickly so you can weather the ebbs and flows and survive the ups and downs of business and life. If you choose to do so, you can increase your chances to achieve a height of success and live a lifestyle of financial freedom that most people will never dream of, those who did not heed these lessons and make these choices.

How do you communicate with your team? Share with us.

QUICK RECAP

Lessons on Being Hands-On:

1. There is no shortcut to success; it requires consistent hard work and getting your hands dirty.
2. Keep your day job as an opportunity to learn how to manage scarce time and to fund your new business.
3. Use your day job as an opportunity to learn skills and lessons that will help you in your business pursuits later.

4. In the beginning, spend more time on your business and less money. Keep your head down and work hard.

5. Fill all roles at your company in the beginning, and as you grow, know all the roles and be familiar with your employees.

6. Create executive summaries as a way of making expectations and visions for a project clear to everyone.

7. Opportunities don't take weekends or holidays off, so integrate your work into every day.

8. Don't trade time and health for wealth. Seek relationships and opportunities to partner and diversify; you will succeed faster and lower your risk.

9. Be all in on everything you do. This will help you juggle all your commitments.

10. Develop and use your street smarts. Keep it simple and sensible.

CHAPTER 6
ESSENTIAL KEY #6
LOOK FOR TEACHABLE MOMENTS

These are moments when you stop, right in the middle of everyone being focused on getting somewhere or something done, and call attention to an important lesson that the situation created.

Back in 2005, when I told my sister that I was ready to launch my own investment firm, she told me to be confident that I would find ways to succeed because I have always been a quick learner. That was an effective use of a teachable moment. These are moments when you stop, right in the middle of everyone being focused on getting somewhere or something done, and call attention to an important lesson that the situation created. You acknowledge that there is a context that will help someone remember what was taught and hopefully learned. In that moment, my sister made me stop and absorb the fact that at times of uncertainty, I should remind myself that I am a quick learner, that I should be confident, start the companies, and keep learning as I go.

In your company, especially early on, use these teachable moments to stop and, in an empathetic way, get your employees to learn something valuable that will make them better. As the CEO, I do not have an office, and I live in Florida, while the company is in Boston. So when I am in the office, I am looking for these teachable moments, especially to show my employees how their daily actions should be tied to our mission, vision, and goals.

How do you effectively conduct a teachable moment? The key is to educate through a conversation, not by shouting commands or berating someone. People prefer if you engage them mentally. I find that by asking questions, I give people the opportunity to figure out the answer and to have their own eureka moment. If I don't use a question, I engage them in connecting the importance of the task at hand to our success. If it is a great opportunity for a lot of employees to learn, I gather the entire company to participate in understanding the teachable subject, without singling out the person who made me initiate the exercise. Many times, that person has the most information anyway and ends up teaching the group. My role is to tie the moment to the business's big picture and success.

Whiteboarding with the group is the most effective method I use to get everyone to realize the teachable subject. It's interesting that over time, my employees have come to yearn for these moments when I am around to go through a whiteboarding exercise or question-and-answer town hall–type gathering. My team invites me out to dinner to discuss important topics, to learn what I am thinking and hear my thoughts about different strategies. More and more, they are doing their own whiteboarding among themselves now, rather than waiting for me to initiate it.

WORK TO RECOGNIZE EFFECTIVE TEACHABLE MOMENTS

The hardest thing for them to grasp is when and what to teach. Not every problem or mistake warrants stopping everyone in their tracks to conduct a teachable moment. Teachable moments are often the product of specific circumstances; they are insights that are difficult to convey memorably during training, because there they lack the unique context that makes them powerful in a certain situation. These are skills that you learn by doing and with experience, so that when the opportunity arises, you can jump on them and shorten the learning curve for an employee or the whole group. As the CEO, you are mostly trying to connect them with how their actions and thinking can affect the business. Managers may use teachable moments to help an employee fit in with the culture of the team, learn how the team works, and impart specific knowledge.

It's important to recognize teachable moments with consistency, so your employees understand that this is part of how you conduct business. These moments should not be so sparse that they think you are just having a bad day or nitpicking. Employees who have worked with me over a long period often tell new employees that I am always watching what everyone is doing, even though I am not around every moment. My executive staff is often surprised when I visit the office, and at the end of the day, I tell them who needs to be fired, who needs a raise, or who needs to be watched and why. This is because I have certain things that I am always looking for from my employees. Many times, it is something they did or said. I connected the dots and concluded that they don't have the company's mission at heart, or they cannot be depended upon, even though they are doing what is asked of them daily. Engage your high performers daily, and the teachable moments will happen easily and frequently. These are the people who want to learn anyway, so they keep getting better. The point is to start developing teachable moments so that when you see the opportunity, you can be more like a coach.

Teachable moments help employees who may be strong-willed in their positions and who are dedicated to getting things done quickly. When you stop them to make a point, and they see the light, it is usually a positive, eye-opening experience. These teachable moments have to be effective at giving them wisdom, not just specific answers. They need to learn insights and nuances of how to look at their actions in the context of the effects on the larger business. If nothing else, I want them to be concerned about what they don't know so that they always have contingency plans. I want them to expect something to go wrong and plan for it as much as they plan for their success.

If you have children, practice teachable moments at home. My kids taught me that learning occurs over time and is best in a real-life context, where it can be repeated and reinforced, so plan to keep jumping on these teachable moments because once is not going to be enough. And remember that when you approach a problem, stop to look into your past to see if you can draw from your reservoir of experience, because no matter where you are in life, you will always have more information behind you than in front of you.

My sister was right; I just have to remember that I am a quick learner and look for teachable moments that I can learn from and then apply what I learned to what is in front of me. Your employees will appreciate that you are always ready to invest in their knowledge growth, and they will be receptive. To ensure that learning becomes a habit for everyone in the companies, I recently instituted a mandatory literature review. This review lets the employees read an article and discuss it so that a perspective outside the company can supplement what we learn every day on the job. My mentor and high school principal, Mr. Chin, once told me there is more danger in a person with some knowledge than a person with no knowledge, because the one with some knowledge will make decisions assuming they know it all. If you are not eager to learn, then no one will teach you, but if you are eager to learn, you will have many teachers and be unstoppable. So be humble and constantly seek knowledge from teachable moments to build your reservoir, which you can draw from in times of decision-making.

My kids taught me that learning occurs over time and is best in a real-life context, where it can be and repeated and reinforced, so plan to keep jumping on these teachable moments because once is not going to be enough.

Have you experienced a teachable moment? Share with us..

QUICK RECAP

Lessons on Teachable Moments:

1. Teachable moments are when you stop everything to call attention to an important lesson created in the situation.
2. Empathetic, teachable moments can help employees connect how their daily actions are tied to the company's vision, mission, and goals.
3. Educate through conversation by mentally engaging someone with questions.
4. Let your questions give people the opportunity to have their own eureka moment.
5. Gather the company around important teachable moments without singling anybody out.
6. Choose teachable moments that focus on helping people understand how their actions affect the business.
7. Managers should use teachable moments to educate employees about team culture and specific knowledge.
8. Use teachable moments consistently, not sporadically.
9. If you have children, practice teachable moments at home.
10. Use storytelling and paint a picture to make your point more memorable.

CHAPTER 7
ESSENTIAL KEY #7
UNDERSTAND THE VALUE OF MONEY .

Treat time and money as if they have equal value.
If you waste time, you are wasting money, and if you waste money,
you are wasting time that you gave up to make the money.

A rich person has money but may not be wealthy. A wealth person has the system and processes that generate money. Ideally you want to be rich while you are building wealth so you don't suffer from lack of money. Usually you get rich from investors giving you money to build wealth in a company. Once you sell the company you are just rich.

Let's agree to not chase money but instead build value, and you will attract money. People pay for value with money. When you have built your value, your worth can be measured in money. Next, you add money by working; you multiply money by investing. People are afraid to invest, so they bank their money in retirement funds, but you must give money in the form of investments to multiply your money. Simple investment mathematics will show billionaires lose billions to make billions; millionaires lose millions to make millions; *thousandaires* lose thousands to make thousands. The message is you have to invest money to make money. This is the lesson of all lessons. I love the saying, "Show me the money!" I never get tired of saying it. When someone pitches an idea to me, I immediately ask them, "Let's cut to the chase. How will you make money?" If they act surprised and start avoiding a direct answer, I tell them I am out. Making money requires an easy-to-understand plan to solve a problem and get paid for it. Without revenue, you don't have customers. Then you don't have a company; you have a hobby, a pastime, or maybe you are focused on research and development (R&D), trying to get your product to the market where it can be sold.

Understanding the value of money is a must, but it's amazing how little we are taught about the value of money at home or in school. I was taught zero about investing money in medical school. Today, many doctors are going to business schools to get a master's in business administration. Although I spent a few years working in business before medical school, and I have been building companies since medical school, I too felt the need for more formal business education. So I also went to business school to study health care management at Miller School of Business at Ball State, and I went to Harvard Business School for the equivalent of a condensed executive master's in business administration as a member of the 2020 class of students in the Program for Leadership Development (PLD31). I don't think we should just blame schools and ignore our parents. Growing up, no one tried to teach me the value of money, so I never understood it; all I knew was "I ain't got none."

I heard J.P. Morgan Sr. gave J.P. Morgan Jr. a bag filled with a million dollars to show him how it felt to hold. And the rest is history. J.P. Morgan Jr. became one of the richest men to ever live, much richer than his father. I make it a point when my children ask me to buy them things, to tell them the cost and ask if they have the money to buy it themselves. I just love the look on their faces when they hold their heads down and whisper, "No." I then say, "I can't hear you. How much money did you say you need to buy it?" I recall my youngest, at two years old, being excited to download free apps on his iPad. My daughter, when she was five years old, was also into the excitement when she found a free app she liked. I make sure they know Daddy is going to work every day to make money so they can have a nice home and nice things. I also recall when we moved into a larger house, my daughter told everyone how we had a small house and now we had a large house; she always ended with, "Thank you, Daddy." When my son was a year and a half, he would point to every white Mercedes Benz and say, "Daddy's car." When he'd go to Chuck E. Cheese, he only wanted to drive fast cars. I think he's going to need a lot of money to feed that habit.

With money, all things become possible. Without it, you are limited, and limitation means your margin for avoiding failure is thin. Your options are fewer, and your ability to weather even a small storm is weakened. Anxiety can set in, and you feel rushed to make short-term decisions. Bottom line: without money, your personal and business life will be very tough, and your dreams might be unrealized. Building a successful business is the best way to make enough money (lots of it) to achieve financial freedom, and once you have it, do whatever you can afford and brings you joy.

But having vast amounts of cash too early in life or too early when starting a business might not be the best situation either. This is why I preach the value of money, not just having it. I've noticed that people without money often develop ideas to make money that do not require a lot of money to invest. Money to them is a necessity, and necessity is the mother of invention, so they find ways to get things done with just enough money. If you have too much money, you think you can buy anything and do anything that comes to mind without deep, thoughtful investigation. With a lot of money, you want to solve problems, so you are looking for ways to spend money. Your ideas can often be grandiose in ways that require large amounts of spending. Everyone around you senses that you have money to spend, and they will gladly help you spend it, rather than looking at ways to help you. If they are employed by you and sense you have money to spend, they won't work as hard as they would if they felt the business depended on their work and not your money.

Once you decide to start your business, the primary money decision should involve three things: how money will come in, how much will you need to build your business on a rolling basis (not just how much to get off the ground), and how much money will be going out (how you can you lose money)?

HOW WILL YOU GET MONEY?

Determining how money will be coming in is the same as identifying the source from which you will get money. To this date, I still hold my day job as an orthopedic spine surgeon, so I have money coming in from my practice. If you can, you should keep a day job to bring in money. This will help you stay hungry while you are building the business, because you have to work harder than if you were only working full-time on your business. This is even more important if you have a family or someone who depends on you financially. You cannot afford to go broke starting a business if others depend on you. As your business grows, you can transition to becoming more full-time there, or tailor your day job to accommodate your business schedule. With today's multimedia technologies and smartphones, you can be a mobile business and be available twenty-four seven while holding a second job.

If you plan to get money from other sources, such as investors, then you need to put together a business plan. If you do go to investors, consider getting a loan before you give away equity. It is better to take debt early on and live within your means to build the business and the equity. Once the company has more value, then you can sell equity for cash. Most entrepreneurs do the opposite; they want to grow big fast and give away the company to early investors in order to shoot out the starting gates and off to the races. It is common to see entrepreneurs flaunting how much money they raised, as if that is the ultimate measure of success of the business. What they later realize is that once you receive funding from investors, you will need to receive more funding and give away more equity. At some point, you wind up working for your investors, on their timelines, with their only mission being to get the most return as fast as possible. If you need investors, get family and friends to invest in the beginning. Or find investors who will help you with the business, not just give you money and sit back. If you are lucky, you may have investors who put in money but also add value in other ways, such as with their business experience, connections, and ability to help you generate more revenues.

Creating an executive summary of your business plan is an important activity and good discipline before you start a business. It's smart to spend your time creating a full business plan, and a formal business plan is necessary for investors. Work with your lawyers to create a private placement memorandum that will be needed for accredited investors to invest in your company while it is private. An accredited investor is someone who has made a salary of at least $200,000 in each of the past two years or whose joint income with a spouse is more than $300,000, with expectations to have the same income in the current year, or has a combined net worth of at least $1 million.

Writing an executive summary and business plan will help you focus on explaining your business to yourself and others in thirty to sixty seconds, or as long as it would take you to be with an investor in an elevator. We started the Healthtech Venture Network Conference (HTVNC) to provide a forum for this type of presentation workshop and created a conference event called ELEVATE. ELEVATE lets entrepreneurs present their ideas in a short time and get feedback. Seek conferences and workshops like this to hone your elevator pitch. Your initial pitch should explain the business in about ten seconds. If you get more time, you can explain how you will make money, what products and services you will offer, at what price, how you will be better than the main competition, how will you scale up the business, and how much money you need. You should outline a road map to lay out how you will spend the money you receive. One of our ten-second pitches goes like this: KICVentures Group is a health care investment company that has built a portfolio of companies with differentiated spine technologies through mergers and acquisitions and intends to go public in 2023.

> Writing an executive summary and business plan will help you focus on explaining your business to yourself and others in thirty to sixty seconds, or as long as it would take you to be with an investor in an elevator.

Remember, you will also need to manage your investors' expectations and personalities. This is a marriage, so there is a risk for a rocky relationship or even a nasty divorce. Carefully determine whose money you take to run your business and outline what their expectations are for getting a return on their investment, including the details of when and how this will happen. Note that beggars are not choosers, so try to get investors when you don't need the money and you are not on the verge of bankruptcy. No one will be excited to invest money to simply keep your business from failing, and if they do invest, they will ask for a large percentage because you need the money to avoid failure. The best time to get investor money is when you have money but see an opportunity to grow your business and solidify its foundation so you are stronger or to get across the finish line and cash out. This time often occurs after five years of having a solid and profitable business.

HOW MUCH MONEY DO YOU NEED?

Avoid getting money in an effort to grow fast early on because you are so sure you know exactly what needs to be done to blow up. This usually happens when someone is still early in the business and sees what might be an opportunity to make a lot of money if they could expand bigger, pivot faster, and enter new markets. This can be a problem because it takes time to really get deep enough to truly understand the market and to build the culture and organization to support moving fast. If you do not have a solid infrastructure or foundation, try to be patient and don't grow fast yet. If you do take money to grow fast without a solid foundation, you will blow through the money just to learn hard lessons. Learn and make mistakes that have small consequences; move fast if you must, but not with a lot of money on the line.

If you have a solid infrastructure and foundation, I encourage you to take on new money, but use it wisely and be prepared to make deals, such as acquisitions and partnerships, to grow your business, rather than racing ahead and spending the money you raised. If you have money and are growing steadily, you will be able to make nimble moves and pull off strategic moves, some of which you will only see if you are patient and not forcing the business. We recently benefited from this strategy by acquiring several entire companies that raced ahead with lots of investor money, ran into trouble when they could not sustain their growth, borrowed money from banks, and eventually fell into foreclosures. We've also had opportunities to invest in great companies because we kept our businesses growing steadily and looked for investments in complementary businesses, rather than trying to spend our money building those businesses. There is no shortage of businesses that will run into financial trouble in your space, and if you are patient and have cash, you will get a lot of great bargains. Most companies don't survive long enough to be in the advantageous position of patiently acquiring other businesses.

I have learned the importance of planning, not just having a plan, before embarking on any venture. You will learn a lot about planning from chalkboarding your ideas with your team and developing a business plan. You will find that the act of planning has prepared your brain to adapt, while the actual plan is more static. Be ready to update your business plan as you go along and learn more. These are the activities that will teach you how to know what your true needs are as they change. Research your industry and constantly try to learn from others, from your competition, and, most importantly, from your customers.

> Research your industry and constantly try to
> learn from others, from your competition, and,
> most importantly, from your customers.

It is important to be the expert at what you do, and the best way to do this is to learn on the job. But this could come at a high price, so also invest in learning off the job. Read books every chance you get and use the internet to have information at your fingertips. In the early stages of starting KICVentures, I had a lot of travel time, so I often bought a book at the airport I could finish reading on my flight. I bought books on areas I needed to improve in. If you are not a great communicator, read books about how to speak or write better. If you don't know how to be a leader, you can learn by reading and implementing what you learn.

I don't suggest getting a degree just to pad your résumé. You are now your own boss; your résumé is your success, and the time value of the money you spend to go back to school might not be worth it. The richest man in the world, Bill Gates, dropped out of Harvard to start Microsoft. Steve Jobs did not have a master's of business administration degree. If you are an entrepreneur, you don't need a degree in administration. However, there are many advantages to advanced degrees, and I do have my share, but I needed those degrees in medicine to know the health care industry as much as possible. I do think advanced education can help you build your formal business intelligence, which is a valuable asset.

Whether or not you should invest the time and money to get an advanced degree depends on your timing and your industry. Also, you must justify the financial impact of the money you will spend on a degree. Once you understand your industry and your business, I don't think getting a degree is a necessity, but it can be a great idea if you feel you can manage your time and not hurt your business. You may find short courses and networking at conferences and tradeshows to be good value for your time. By believing in yourself and pursuing learning constantly, you will develop street smarts from what you read, what you apply, and what you test; you will eventually figure out what does and does not work. Whether you have a degree or not, time is money, and in order for your business to thrive, you must spend your time learning about your customers and your business and working with others on the front line, not closed up in a fancy office. I am on the road overnight an average of three nights per week. The more time I spend on the front lines, the more I learn and the more relationships I build that can bring in investors and customers.

HOW MONEY WILL BE GOING OUT

You will need to save money, so start by making use of what is free or cheap. In 1999, when I started Meduweb (our medical distance learning company), I renovated the basement of our house in Cambridge. It was rent-free and only cost us a nominal fee to renovate. When the market crashed in 2000, we did not have a long-term, expensive lease to worry about; we just closed down the business and used the basement for other things. I made my first million dollars in real estate, buying and upgrading condominiums in Cambridge while

I was a resident at Harvard. I had a small hatchback Honda Civic, and I used it to transport material and tools between Home Depot and the condominiums we renovated. I spent very little on gas, and we did not need to buy a new vehicle for the business.

Early on as an entrepreneur, I spent too much before I realized that building a business is an evolution and a journey that takes place over time. In the beginning, you will make a lot of mistakes and experience growing pains, just as I did, especially if you throw a lot of money at starting your business. Keep your spending down, and be patient as you gain experience and learn how to spend your money more effectively. Understand that it takes time. I recommend that you tell yourself you plan to own your business for ten years, so that your decisions to spend money are not rushed. Be honest with investors and do not overpromise on timelines; if you're going to overpromise, do so on the vision of what you will accomplish, as it's better to surprise them with an earlier than expected return on their investment. Just because you plan to run your business for ten years does not mean you have to wait that long to return an investment, but you may have to.

You will have short-term goals, but it is also important to always have a long-term strategy. This is important not just financially but also for the character of the company. There will be times when you hold onto your money because it benefits your long-term strategy. Delayed gratification, when it comes to finances, is something to strive for in business. Have the foresight to not spend money un-wisely so you can meet your long-term goals.

> Investing and waiting on long-term goals develops
> patience, and patience develops character.

A lesson on taxes is very important to heed. To get tax benefits, you have to spend money, so don't get suckered into spending freely because you might get some tax benefits. Every year, when our taxes get calculated at KICVentures, we are dismayed by the amount of our profits that go toward taxes. You too will be hit with taxes, so allocate the money to pay them. Do not spend your cash, and don't forget that the tax department always collects, even in death. If you think you can hide money and avoid taxes by putting your business under a family name, get a tax lawyer instead. You need to fully understand these potential havens before you start spending money and thinking you will benefit by lowering your taxes.

As for putting your business under family names—worse, under your spouse's—I do not recommend this since it's well accepted that family and business do not mix well, and relationships change. Before you do anything with the intention of avoiding taxes or defrauding the government, remember that intentions cannot be hidden behind legal and tax maneuvers, and intentions are as bad as what law you actually break.

As you build your team, remember to keep the group small and working in close physical proximity. Avoid a lot of office space and high rents with long terms. You should be doing most of the work anyway. Staff within your means. No more than 40 to 50 percent of your profits should be spent on staffing. Avoid the temptation to let pride creep in and increase your staff because you want to look successful, or you want to feel more like the boss and less like you are one of the workers.

At some point, when you have built the foundation to take on customers on a larger scale, plan to get the word out as cheaply and effectively as possible. Building your brand is building trust. I think this is like starting all over again, because now you are ready to grow, and growth requires cash. This could bankrupt you if you are in a business that requires a lot of inventory purchases, and your collections could be delayed. KICVentures' medical device companies have to be careful with accelerating growth, as this is highly risky because we need to spend a lot on inventory, sales representatives, and commissions, and we have to wait for hospitals to pay us. This sales cycle means that our inventory returns a profit only after a certain amount of utilization, and in that window, we could run out of money. Account for all these potential issues as you grow. In the first phase of your branding, get your team to do most of the work; find creative ways to utilize the internet and any means you can to get the word out without spending yourself into a tight cash position.

You should also keep in mind how you can lose money. The first lesson on losing money is how you manage your personal love relationships. The number one rule I use is this: you can lose a lot of money chasing personal relationships, but you will not have a shortage of personal relationships if you chase money. History is filled with stories of rich and successful people falling in love and losing a lot of money. Ask any person how they feel when half their fortune disappears after a divorce. Look around at your employees before they fall in love and after. You cannot serve two masters, and love is one of the strongest masters and very jealous. You can waste more money and time chasing relationships for love, faster than any other way I know of, and you will enjoy it so much you won't care until it is too late.

The hormonal response to love is like drugs; it is fast acting, irresistible once you indulge it, and intoxicating, clouding all your judgment unless you love money and success more. Everything you do in the name of love seems justified while you have money to support your emotions, like drugs. Work takes time away from your relationship, both mentally and physically, unless you have the proper perspective and are in control of yourself. Do not start your business fifty-fifty with a lover or spouse; it will be the death of your relationship and your company. Plus, your employees will always see it as a family business and not theirs to share.

Like everything in life, there are exceptions, but don't follow exceptions as the rule. If you are going to fall in love, first fall in love with your desire to succeed, so you don't fall off track. If you follow this rule, then love is the honey of life. With the money you will have and the business behind your money to sustain your lifestyle, love as much as you want and have the time of your life. You were warned.

Having said this, there is a healthy way to integrate your desire to succeed and your business pursuits with your personal relationships. Money without someone you love to share it with or love without money to afford the bounties and diverse experiences of this beautiful world should be strongly avoided. If you get too deep in money pursuits or love pursuits, either can lead to an unhappy place. Because of this, I have always picked my serious partner to be someone who literally shares the journey. I find it is true the family that prays and plays together stays together. If you are all about yourself, you will end up all by yourself on your big, fat yacht and trolling in your fancy car, but it will all be superficial. My wife travels with me on business trips and shares in the day-to-day knowledge of what is happening with all my businesses. I bring my kids on business trips as often as I can schedule them around their school. I keep my extended family in the know as well, to varying degrees. Success is a journey to be shared and enjoyed by everyone you care about by making time for people along the way. Keep it simple and sensible, and stay hungry and humble.

The more money you have, the more money you waste. Of course, this is a personal decision, and it is your money to do with as you want. But I encourage you to resist the urge to spend on yourself too early. I believe you can tell a lot about a company by looking at how the owners live their personal lives. I admire the very rich who still enjoy the simple things in life and do not show off their wealth.

In order to stay grounded and hungry, I paid rent for the formative years of my companies, and I still lease my car and mix my family trips with business trips. Visits to fancy restaurants are mostly reserved for business. I told myself that only when I felt the time was right would I purchase a house, and since starting KICVentures in 2005, I waited ten years to buy a home. A house is a fixed investment with no immediate return. It sucks your money and can lull you into a state of complacency. Cash flow is a significant weapon, so create cash flow and protect it.

In 2014, we acquired AxioMed LLC, a company that makes a unique viscoelastic total disc replacement for the cervical and lumbar spine. We did this deal under a state of emergency, within three days of hearing about the foreclosed asset sale by the bank. AxioMed had $70 million in venture capital funding, plus bank loans, yet it ran out of money. A bank took over the assets and put the company into foreclosure. We had access to cash for this emergency purchase and still had enough to keep the business running. If we did not have the cash, we would not have been able to purchase this company. So you cannot afford to be cash poor.

Having said this, I don't believe you should sit around on cash when you could be reinvesting to make more. You have to spend money to make money. You cannot sit scared on money; you must learn the value of money and account for every penny.

DO NOT HOARD; LET MONEY FLOW

From a young age, I remember hearing stories about people who succeeded and how success changed them. Their old friends would discuss how much they'd changed. In Jamaica, they say, "He got rich and switched," meaning he changed his values. It's easy for the successful people to call these old friends haters or accuse them of jealousy. So who is right? Does success have to change you as a person? To me, it's a matter of remembering where you come from. When you decide to start a business, you quickly realize that help is hard to come by; some people you know have the money or the knowledge to help but choose not to. This can be a very difficult lesson for some entrepreneurs to learn and accept. You'll work extremely hard to get loans, to create deals, and to make your dream a reality. If you are equal parts fortunate and smart, and you manage to succeed, I urge you to remember how it felt when you needed help. Think back to when you had nothing, when you were struggling to make it, and just how valuable some financial assistance would have been. If you remember your roots and use your money to reinvest into creating more wealth for yourself and others, I believe your experiences and network will be just as valuable, if not more so, as money.

I think the haters have some valid points about getting rich and switching. It's easy to take your wealth and hoard it in a high-yield account, and everyone is entitled to use their hard-earned money as they see fit. But I believe you should reach out and help others by putting your money to work for you and for them. I don't believe in hoarding your money or being afraid to lose it. You see this all the time. Wealthy people begin to self-indulge, receding further into their own riches, and they stop seeing opportunities to build relationships, however opportune those relationships could be.

I think you do yourself a disservice if you only indulge yourself on material things, building a wall around you and your wealth because you are too busy to find time for others who might be asking for your help. But if you remember your own journey and give back to the future generations, you will find that your experiences are richer than your bank account. The more money you have, the more money you should spend on other people. This is why I started KICVentures, so I could invest money in great ideas and especially in the people I know. I see us in every major city, finding new entrepreneurs to fund.

Back in 2013, Michael, the creative director of SpineFrontier, approached me with a novel idea. He pitched a head-up display, which mounts to your car's dashboard and leverages the power of your smartphone to deliver messaging, social media, music, and navigation, completely hands-free and voice activated. The project would be expensive and challenging, but it could change the way people communicate in their cars, and it could end distracted driving to help save lives from car accidents. He told me about the financial toll on him and his family and said it was distracting him from performing his best at anything. I could see that he believed in this idea and that he was at a crossroads, without many resources to continue with the idea.

> The opportunity we seized out of adversity may never have existed. To me, that's far more valuable than a big number on a monthly financial statement. Remember, investing in others and ideas can be rewarding in ways that are more than merely financial.

I saw a spark in Michael, so I evaluated the idea and quickly realized that this was an immensely valuable opportunity if I were to dedicate my time and money to help. Today, that idea has come to fruition in the form of our company SenseDriver Technologies. The first hardware product is SenseHUD, a head-up display for safer driving, which works in conjunction with SenseSay, the app that powers the platform using your mobile device. We have assembled a great software team and are about to release SenseSay, fully integrated with voice command, for apps like WhatsApp, so whether you're driving or are outside your vehicle, you will be able to command your phone using voice commands for key functions like phone calls, texting, and navigation. We also spun off a new hardware device for surgeons to use in the operating room called SenseScope, to replace expensive and cumbersome microscopes. Just when we thought we had made all the right changes, the market opportunity for SenseHUD and SenseSay was no longer there for us to pursue. By this time, we had a great software team. We had our drive and our belief in persevering.

One day, I was in the clinic when the idea of using voice-activated software in medicine rather than in a car came to me. I also saw the vast potential of social media as a way to create one global medical digital engagement community as the next social media for medical information. This is how we decided to covert the SenseSay software into a new company called MediConnects. We were excited, as this would immediately solve problems we have with scheduling patient appointments and having them fill out all their forms with a medical history. This would lead to having meaningful interactions with the patients online. As we built the software, we noticed that the functionality we needed to make it user friendly started to resemble other platforms. Features such as uploading content, comments, and connection and that the profile features would be equivalent to maintaining the medical records of a patient.

The excitement was building, as we felt that we were on the verge of a true revolution in developing a collaborative platform between patients and medical providers; given the similarities to the medical provider platform, it could be easily adopted. So there we were, thinking we had a sure thing, and we believed it was what we should bring to the market.

But as we have learned, the only surety in the technology space is change. As we were building out the software, we saw the need for an enterprise-grade collaborative platform for all organizations, not only medicine; as such, Neetworkiin was born. The company name is Afrikaans for "networking." LinkedIn admitted they have a network gap for the people who needed networking the most. Neetworkiin aims to fill the network gap.

We have forged great strategic partners from Boston to Silicon Valley, India, and China, and along the way, we witnessed experiences much more valuable than if the money was sitting in an account somewhere. I watched Michael grow into a confident businessman. This is a priceless joy for me and those around him who witnessed his transition. Had I hoarded my wealth, avoided the risk, and left him without financial resources and mentorship, MediConnects and Neetworkiin might never have been born. The opportunity we seized out of adversity may never have existed. To me, that's far more valuable than a big number on a monthly financial statement. Remember, investing in others and ideas can be rewarding in ways that are more than merely financial.

How do you value money? Share with us on

QUICK RECAP

Lessons on the Value of Money:

1. Read and learn about the value of money before you get it or lose it.
2. Know how much money will come in, go out, and be necessary for building your business.
3. Build a business plan to guide you and for investors, and have a thirty-second elevator pitch ready.
4. Don't give away equity too early. Take on debt. When you have value, sell equity for cash.
5. Build your value to attract money and invest to multiply your money.
6. Be frugal by using the resources you already have.
7. Plan for taxes.
8. Staff within your means and keep your office space to the necessary minimum.
9. Rich is having money. Wealth is having processes and systems that create a flow of money
10. Don't hoard your money; gain valuable experience by investing in others.

CHAPTER 8
ESSENTIAL KEY #8

YOUR TIME IS YOUR GREATEST RESOURCE

> If you have some money but not a lot, spend
> more time and less money. If you have a lot of
> money, spend more money and less time.

A ging past fifty years old will likely stimulate you to look closely at how you spend your time. For those younger than fifty, don't wait; start now to value your time. If you can stop wasting time, it means you will have more time to use wisely, and this means more time for you to pursue your dreams and vision while doing meaningful things that will contribute to your happiness and fulfillment. My best time-management technique is to block time to work with a small team to complete a task. I used to have a to-do list, but blocking time for the key tasks for the day ensures I complete the task that our team blocked off time for. Another technique is to set your schedule each morning so that you have to complete those activities before you open your day for other things that are changeable. So every morning at 8:15, I have a team call with my executive team. This is my meeting, so I must be there. My next technique is to avoid people who waste your time or activities that waste your time, such as watching television. Next is to avoid meaningless activities. We've all heard the saying "Time is money." So if we waste time, we waste money. But is time just about money? What about the value of time itself?

Everything we do has a finite time associated with it—everything. Everything you do has an expiration date, so I make sure that the time I invest will have meaningful and lasting benefits so that when the time runs out and I move on, I take the value with me. Take golf. I invested thousands of hours in golf, but today I rarely play golf. When I do play, usually with business friends, I maintain the fundamentals I learned when I played a lot of golf. I just don't have the time or the desire today to play a lot of golf. I've often wondered whether golfers would play more often and the sport would make more money if we were to change the game from eighteen to sixteen holes. What if everyone on the course wore a timer that the clubhouse monitored and used to move people along? What if we infused time of play into the scoring? If I putt out slower than the timer for that hole allows, I lose a stroke. Why not? We shortened boxing from fifteen rounds to twelve and made the necessary adjustment in our expectations.

I also question the eight-hour workday. I just don't believe this is enough time to be truly productive. I wonder how many eight-hour days it would have taken to build the great pyramids, the Hoover Dam, or any great structure. Carnegie ran his steel mills twenty-four seven to meet the demand and industrialize the world to create massive wealth. How many billions of people are sitting around underproductive, with no jobs and nothing to do?

Take the classic scenario of a typical workday. A lot of us get to work, and the first hour is spent just trying to finish our coffee to get our minds ready to work. An hour before noon, we are already planning our one-hour lunch. After we eat, we use the first hour to get back into work, just in time to be thinking about leaving at five o'clock. Ask what we do with the other sixteen hours, and you will find a lot of wasted time, watching television and talking on the phone, not to mention surfing the internet or trying to please other people by living their lifestyles. I don't believe any of this is premeditated; it's just that the system is not set up for us to be efficient with our time.

I imagine the future with cameras and monitors everywhere to watch our movements. How would this affect us? Big Brother could call us out for being unproductive. This does not mean we would all be working all the time, just that the state may not allow us to waste time. Do talented, able-bodied people have the right to waste time? Did Einstein have an obligation to the state to use his genius more than he did? If Einstein were alive, what would he say if you asked him if he wished he had done more with his time?

I will step up and say, if given the choice for us to be monitored, I would take the deal. It would be great to have someone kicking me in the butt to get going when I am slacking. I would not complain if, in the end, I got to do more every day, including have more time and the means to have fun. I would even change from a twenty-four-hour to a thirty-hour day to be more productive and efficient. You would have more daylight time to enjoy yourself. And splitting work between daytime and nighttime is a much better deal in my book. I have never been to Alaska, but it is fascinating to think of the possibilities there, in the land of the midnight sun.

If we removed money as a currency, I believe time would be a better replacement. If time were the currency, we would not want to waste it as easily as we might waste money, and we would all be more aware of our own biological clocks. I bet we would be more effective in everything we did if we used time as a currency. Wouldn't you want to gain more time? Can you imagine how hard people would work to accumulate time to live longer?

Of course, this idea is just for the movies. But what if we could train ourselves to act as if time were precious, like our currency? Or what if we could train ourselves to imagine Big Brother was watching us to see how much time we wasted? In both these cases, I would immediately want to achieve the shortest path to success. Wouldn't you? Your success and your company's success ultimately depends on time management: how well you manage it, how your actions and decisions affect your team's time, and how effectively your team spends its time.

So how do you remind yourself to make the best use of your time? The key to time management is to plan before you act. Get the knowledge you need, begin with earnest, and drive hard to the finish line on all your tasks. Pace yourself if you must, but there is plenty of time to slow down after you succeed—not till then. Be tenacious, do the best job now, and be reliable. You can practice this every day by writing down your to-do list and holding yourself accountable for it.

Divide your to-do list into tasks that are time fillers, that you can do without much thinking, the ones that just need to get done. Then there are tasks that are critical, the must-do tasks that you must finish before the end of the day (and I don't mean workday; I mean the twenty-four-hour day). These are tasks that often require you to be focused, to think, and to strategize because you are the lead architect in charge of getting them done. When tasks come up during the day, you put them into one of these categories. Some of your tasks are really other people's tasks that you are pulled into, but I still consider these fillers.

I go even further than to-do lists and write an executive summary of every important job that my team and I will tackle. This summary gives me an understanding of why I want to do the job, the potential problems we need to solve, and what resources will be necessary. It also lists individual tasks at the ones and zeros level and a timeline for the completion of each task and the overall job. I find that when I share this executive summary with the team, they have a better road map, versus when we just discuss things verbally. Plus, the team can also have the confidence that they know exactly what I need from them because it is written down. This reminds me of the Chinese proverb, a promise is only as good as the paper it is written on.

Since I started using executive summaries, I have broadened their use to repurpose each employee's job description. The job description is now written as an executive summary, with a background on the company as the employee understands it, the employee's personal mission to help the company, the vision of where they see themselves going in the company, the problems they see affecting the company that their job can solve, and a proposal of those solutions. The executive summary outlines what resources they will need, what goals they will set, and what tasks will be needed to achieve those goals in a predetermined timeline.

This is a big-picture executive summary, versus the executive summary for a specific project, but there are similarities. For example, as the CEO of KICVentures, I see the company's mission is to revolutionize health care through innovative technologies and services to treat patients. My mission is to find the best people and build a working team to ensure the company is driving hard to be on the cutting edge. I envision our company and myself as CEO being recognized as the leading provider of health care technologies, having LESS Institute treatment centers and LES Clinics in every city on the globe, and bringing surgeons and patients together under our brand and on an internet platform. Our key problems are to build these LESS Institutes and develop the technologies and products the surgeons and patients will want.

How do we overcome the dominance of hospitals and attract the best doctors to get patients to come to our outpatient ambulatory surgery centers instead of hospitals? Our solutions include developing medical device companies and other superior technologies that patients will want. We also need to develop our online software companies, Neetworkiin and Mediconnects, to have rich algorithmic content and membership opportunities for both surgeons and patients to connect with one another. We set goals like developing a prototype, three-story, 90,000-square-foot LESS Institute with six operating rooms, as a full-service outpatient hospital in Florida and Kingston, Jamaica. We will eventually replicate this in all major cities and invite doctors to participate in ownership and use of the facility. We're doing this because we believe we can deliver higher quality and affordable health care to more people globally than the current hospital paradigm does.

Executive summaries are tools for time management that can help you on the path to success. So remember, if you succeed, but it took longer than it needed to and you did not give it your best time and 100 percent effort, it will diminish the satisfaction of the success. If you fail, you are left with the eternal regret that you might have succeeded had you spent your time differently and given it more effort. The very people who helped you use up your time will also have their opinions about why you failed, and it will not be because of them.

If you are leading a team, you must manage your time to ensure that you are supervising your team's work appropriately and that there are systems and processes in place to allow maximum results with the minimal effort in the shortest amount of time. I developed a formula to ensure I follow this lesson. It shows that the result is dependent on putting the maximum effort upfront and on maximally supervising the team with the least amount of effort because you instituted systems, processes, and strategies.

So remember, if you succeed, but it took longer than it needed to and you did not give it your best time and 100 percent effort, it will diminish the satisfaction of the success. If you fail, you are left with the eternal regret that you might have succeeded had you spent your time differently and given it more effort.

$$\text{Results} = \frac{k \times \text{maximum supervision}}{\text{minimal effort}}$$

$$k = \text{upfront effort}$$

Use your upfront effort to establish systems, processes, and strategies and to train your team so that you know what to supervise in order to get the best results with the least amount of effort. If you find yourself putting a lot of time and effort into supervising, you don't have good systems and processes in place, and there's a lack of clear strategies; you will be too busy trying to get things done by micromanaging. When you have great systems, all work will be maximally supervised, there will be checks and balances and protocols to follow, and you'll expend less effort in doing the actual supervising. To get the best results, you need the most supervising with the least effort.

The ultimate is to have an assembly line preprogrammed with no human being working on it, so every action is micromanaged by a computer program; you, as the manager, just have to flip a switch to turn on the assembly line. If you don't heed this formula, you will not have the time to be open to new opportunities because you'll be too preoccupied. It's better to make time upfront to invest in getting everyone fully knowledgeable, to define their roles, and to ensure they are working as effectively as they can. Define the key strategies and tasks and have the right people employed on your team. This is building your system, developing processes, and training the team. After doing all this work at the outset, you will find you have a lot more personal time afterward. Once this is in place, everyone needs to know they must drive hard to the finish line on every task and give 100 percent, no less.

How do you maximize your time? Share with us.

QUICK RECAP

Lessons on Time:

1. Train yourself to be reminded that your time in life is fixed; once gone, it is gone, so give 100 percent to achieve your goal or don't attempt it.
2. Being too busy with yourself could mean you miss important opportunities in life and business.
3. Look at every opportunity to determine how to most effectively spend your time. Time wasted can be money wasted.
4. Time is a continuum; it is the same time whether you are at work or home, so enjoy work, play, and family maximally.
5. Be available twenty-four seven, or you will spend more time fixing problems later when you choose to be available.
6. Invest maximum time upfront in building effective supervision systems to create more free time in the future.
7. Procrastination is the enemy of success, so act urgently when you see an opportunity because the window of opportunity often closes quickly.
8. Plan what you will do with every minute of your day; even rest and recreation time should work to benefit you in a measurable way.
9. Prioritize your team's time above your personal time so they can keep working with your help; this will free up more of your time later.
10. Poor use of time and lack of knowledge are why companies fail, while running out of money is how they ultimately fail.

CHAPTER 9
ESSENTIAL KEY #9
FAIL FAST AND MAKE ADJUSTMENTS;
DON'T TRY TO BE PERFECT

One of the most important things you can make is
a mistake that you can solve, learning something
that you would not have known otherwise.

I f you want to overcome failure, just keep trying and make adjustments with each attempt. I learned this lesson from a conversation
I had about basketball. The person I was talking with said if you
want to correct missed shots, keep taking shots. Michael Jordan
is famously known for taking shots and not worrying about what
percentage he completed. He missed more potential winning shots
than he scored winning shots. The human spirit has no boundaries;
this is evident by how the world changes by leaps and bounds every
decade due to our ingenuity. We are finding ways to solve problems our predecessors did not fully understand or did not have the
necessary resources to address. The point is whatever you are doing
today, have the humility to know that whatever solution you find,
someone likely will have a better one soon. You therefore cannot
afford to move too slowly, trying to overthink every move you make

and perfect every product you develop. The idea is to plan quickly and move urgently to execute your plan, without fear of failing or making mistakes. If you move slowly and make mistakes, you have less chance of recovering because you might have missed the window of opportunity to make corrections, and situations are always changing. You have to do your research and understand the opportunity and risks. Then you move quickly and make adjustments as mistakes arise. I see it this way: plan in motion, decide in motion, test in motion, fail in motion, correct in motion, and cycle back as often as possible until you get it right.

I am often told I like to gamble and take risks, and I am always in a rush. Truth be told, I don't gamble; I don't even invest in the stock market because I don't have the time to understand the ups and downs of it. I don't even believe I take risks; what I do is evaluate my moves and their consequences and then develop a process to achieve my goal and have contingencies. I don't see risk; I see steps, and I am quick to learn fast and adjust and keep trying.

I am never in a rush; anyone who knows me will tell you I will sit with you as long as needed, like nothing else is going on, because I am always in the moment, trying to see things that require my attention to the end. I am the guy who invested fifteen years in medical school to complete residency, fellowship, and four years in academics before moving to Florida to start my private practice. I believe if you want to go far, you must walk slowly, or if you want to build fast, you must build slowly so you avoid big mistakes and having to reverse your journey, ultimately slowing you down.

I do get overbooked trying to fit in as much as I can, so I end up being late to meetings with people, but the reality is I make the meetings count and am quick to apologize for being late. I see problems, and I see opportunities to solve them, plus ways to innovate as I go hard and fast before someone does it in place of me. I am also not afraid to make a mistake or fail. But because mistakes and failures do happen frequently, I avoid going for home runs and look more for base hits and bunts, scrapping to put up points and ultimately win the game.

Achieving the goal is what counts in the end, not so much how fast you get there. I was recently trying to work out a win-win deal, and the other party kept saying they didn't believe I had the abilities to execute; therefore, they wanted the deal to be their way or no way. They had lost sight of the final goal and were getting caught up in the fear of failure. It was not what they thought of my abilities that mattered; it was our commitment to the goal, finding ways to move quickly and adjust along the way. They were negotiating with me because I owned the company. It did not matter how I came to own the company; what mattered was doing the deal and working together to succeed. If you doubt my ability, then you lend your expertise to get us across the finish line, because talking about failure won't help. One of the most important things you can make is a mistake that you can solve, learning something that you would not have known otherwise. Mistakes that are due to sloppy effort waste time but are still teaching moments for you to improve on your business.

> Sometimes people are so afraid of making mistakes that in the process of avoiding failure, they also avoid success.

Failures and mistakes are inevitable, especially when you begin your first business venture; you have very little experience and will definitely make mistakes. Better to set many goals and fail small and frequently than rarely but spectacularly with devastating consequences. Sometimes people are so afraid of making mistakes that in the process of avoiding failure, they also avoid success. So be proactive in creating a culture of product before perfection, so your team moves quickly and decisively to get your product out the door, ready to adapt if there is a problem.

This culture also teaches your employees to be measured in their expectations, so they don't make big mistakes. I remember having a senior supply chain manager. I must admit I was too hands-off early on because of her experience, and I did trust her judgment. This was early in our company's development, so when we found out she had given the OK to order five hundred pieces of an implant that our engineers were still designing, with feedback still coming in from the field, we knew we had made a huge mistake. Over four years later, we are still improving the design on this implant, based on feedback from our customers. The original five hundred pieces sat for years, until recently we were able to resurrect this device into a new market. In the long term, it turned out to be fortuitous, but we lost money for years with the implants sitting around. However, we learned from this mistake and understand that our customer needs will always change and that we should move quickly to adapt and be measured in how we plan to sell our products to the market. If demand outstrips our supply, that is a good problem to have; we just have to be prepared to move quickly to fill the demand. It's better to anticipate the demand by staying close to our customers.

REVIEW PROGRESS EARLY AND OFTEN

In pursuit of perfection, we often waste time that would have been better spent making corrections. I constantly tell my employees to show me what they are working on. If they are going to fail to meet the demands of the project, they might as well do so in the beginning rather than waiting until the end. Look for people who tell you they are "working on it," and stop them and say, "Let's do it now." Beware of employees who tell you they have it under control and things are flowing on schedule. They will also tell you how they did it before in other companies and ask you to trust them.

Immediately stop them and go over their daily schedule. Ask tough business questions. In their mind, the project might be on track based on their timelines. But did they account for things going wrong in areas not under their control? Did they plan for contingencies? Do they keep track of the day-to-day changes in other areas of the company that could affect them? I tell my team to expect to have a problem 100 percent of the time with anything they do for the first time. If they are using a manufacturer that has never made the product before, expect something to go wrong. If they have never worked with a material before, expect something to go wrong. If they are relying on someone to do something for the project, expect something to go wrong and manage that person closely.

The employees I trust the most and who do the best are paranoid; they look for how things can go wrong, and they are hands-on and do things now, not later. If you don't focus on knowing every detail about what you are working on, and if you don't execute your plan in a timely manner, then if something can go wrong, you have opened the door for it to go wrong, and it will. This is a simple point; you can go ahead and call it Murphy's law. You must also plan ahead of time to deal with problems when things go wrong. Invest in determining how to identify problems. My worst employees try to complete the project without getting feedback, because they feel they know what needs to be done, and they will show me they can do it. These are the employees who take the longest to accomplish projects, because they aim to do it as perfectly as possible on their own. They will confront you to defend their positions and to reassure you that they understand what needs to be done.

As the head of the company, you must know what you are looking for from your employees and keep the business interests of the company at the forefront of your decisions. You should be able to tell them whether they're meeting your expectations or not. Many employees don't know all the business goals like you do, so tell them and connect goals and consequences to what they do. They need to put maximum effort into every project upfront so they can fail quickly in the beginning and avoid wasting time later in the process. Build in time for them to present their ideas early on, understanding that they will most likely need to make adjustments. If they succeed, then you are already ahead of schedule and better off for having put aside that time.

What is the most important lesson you've learned from failure? Share with us.

QUICK RECAP

Lessons on Failing Fast:

1. Better to fail earlier than later so you can make quick adjustments upfront.
2. Expect to fail over and over before you get it right.
3. Only by trying will you beat a failure.
4. Only by studying failure will you learn and get better.
5. Move urgently and don't be afraid to make mistakes.
6. Create a culture of putting products before perfection and adapt if a problem arises.
7. Review progress early and often and help employees think through potential problems.
8. Help employees connect larger business goals with the consequences of what they do.
9. Encourage employees to complete tasks immediately rather than waiting to perform them perfectly.
10. Manage your employees with a daily to-do list.

CHAPTER 10
ESSENTIAL KEY #10
BE CUSTOMER FOCUSED

> When thinking about your businesses purpose and
> mission, it should be centered around satisfying
> the customer, not just your dreams.

S uccessful businesses rely on the customer. A product is created, or service offered, that can be marketed to people to satisfy a desire or solve a problem. Without the customer focus, your reason for the business to exist is misguided, and everyone will see through the façade. Customers pay to make your business run. Think about it: if you are not happy with a business, you will not buy from them. Customers, as a rule, buy from people and businesses they trust and respect. Therefore, everything you do for your business should be done with the customer in mind, to build your brand to be trusted and respected for your product quality and service delivery. It's all about the customer.

Most people at some point in their lives think about starting their own company. They look around and see other people succeeding at their companies, and they want the same. Instead of seeing the customers in the business and how much the business is serving the customer by solving their problems, they want to have a company to be the boss, to come and go as they please, and to have their name as the company name. When you were a child, you might have dreamed big, before the realities of life stole your dreams. Or it might have begun as you got older and had enough of following someone else's agenda or being broke. Really, at any point, you might just have the itch to be the boss. If you decide to take the steps to build a business, you quickly learn of critics, skeptics, and haters who don't believe in you, but it's your job to prove to both them and yourself that you can do it. These reasons may all work to motivate you, but if you're creating a company to please only yourself and think of the customer as just the means to an end, it will fail.

When thinking about your business's purpose and mission, it should be centered around satisfying the customer, not just your dreams. Choose a mission statement that reflects satisfying the customer better than any other company can. Your brand will be your promise of quality and trust to the customer, and your product is the customer experience. The product is not what you sell. You sell what you stand for and to satisfy the customer's wants and needs, and the product is what customers consume and pay for. If the product fulfills your promise to satisfy their wants and needs, you will have a thriving business.

It is important that you do not oversell yourself because customers don't want to be sold to; they want to be empowered to make the choice themselves. Find a way to connect with your customer. Break the ice in some way and get people to trust you, respect you, and like you before you try to sell them anything. I cannot repeat it enough: people buy from those they trust, like, and respect. My car salesman does not sell cars; he has relationships. And I am one of his customers, not just someone who buys cars from him. He calls me out of the blue to connect me with people he feels I can do business with. And I just like the guy; he is a nice person and always makes time for me. I feel he has integrity and honesty, so I respect and like him as well. No wonder I keep getting these two-year leases and changing my car, enjoying the experience all the while.

Think about managing your early customer relationships at the start of your company with your time, not just throwing money around into outsourcing marketing and hiring distributors. In the beginning stages of your company, you need to take the time to get to know your customers. Everyone has their first customer; make the effort to actually talk to them and gain their feedback.

My first patient in my Fort Lauderdale office gave me a dollar bill and said, "I know you are going to do well. I want you to remember me by this dollar bill I am giving you as your first payment for taking care of me." I still remember him and his thoughtfulness in connecting with me at such a personal level. In Jamaica, I routinely go to patients' homes to change their surgical site dressings. I sit and break bread with them and their families. I give them my personal phone number and say I am available if they need me. I even wrote a paper to demonstrate that patients love to have their doctor's cell phone number and do not call unnecessarily. In fact, our study found the times they called their doctors to always be for legitimate reasons.

When my patients call me, I am always glad and take care of the matter quickly. This saves the patient from waiting too long to get treated and thus avoids problems. It is a privilege to have customers, and the least we should do is show them our appreciation and care. So give your undivided attention to the customer experience and work with them in a way that will give you valuable insight into how you can improve your service. This is not about telling them what you have to offer but rather listening to them as they reveal whether your promise met their expectations or not.

I admire people who start a restaurant and spend all day and night there for the first few years, making sure they meet the customers' needs. I have seen them work directly with every employee to check the quality of the meals and manage the details that, if overlooked, could kill their restaurants. I think about how building the LESS Institute as a solo orthopedic and spine surgeon was all about the people along the way. I started with one employee who filled every role needed to keep an office running. We treated every patient who walked through our doors with the utmost care and attention, and we gave them all our time. We hired a young medical assistant, just out of school, who was affordable and moldable to our culture. We slowly added more employees as my practice increased, and in 2014, we grew to more than forty employees and treated more than two thousand new patients.

The results? Our revenues have grown substantially year over year, and we have very high patient satisfaction scores. I tell my staff that they are there to help me give the same care I give to each of my patients, as if it were just me alone. If my patients have a bad experience, they will tell me personally, because they know I will listen. While an employee might overlook their feelings, I will not. This is another benefit of giving patients my cell phone: they take my business success personally and help me improve. Why? Because my success means they will continue to have access to a quality experience.

I trained a concierge team called Surgical Education Relationship Value and Empathy (SERVE) that helps me manage the hands-on customer relationships, so my patients rarely need to call me. Your customers are your greatest marketers; they tell your story better than you can, and other customers are more likely to take their advice or testimonials.

> Your customers are your greatest marketers; they tell your story better than you can, and other customers are more likely to take their advice or testimonials.

The lesson is win over your customers with the promise of a great product and trusted service and be someone they like. Why is your product or service better than your competition? You and your customers should answer this question with enthusiasm.

USE YOUR STORY TO CONNECT WITH CUSTOMERS

> You have to believe your own story; you cannot
> effectively sell what you don't believe.

One of the most effective ways to capture an audience of customers is to tell your story. Why did you build a company, and what are you trying to accomplish with your products and services that make you different? What do you stand for? You have to believe your own story; you cannot effectively sell what you don't believe. In 2006, when I decided to form our medical device company, I believed as a spine surgeon I was the most capable person to get the best team to design surgical instruments and medical devices for spine surgery. Why not believe you are the best? I was doing the surgeries and following the patients to see how they responded to the treatments, so I was getting firsthand experience that I converted to knowledge. This is why it's best to start a business in an area that you know very well and are passionate about.

Before I started SpineFrontier, I was using the products of other medical device companies, but I did not like how they were made or how I was treated as a customer. I also saw that the patients who were my customers were not doing as well as I wanted with the current technologies and techniques, despite my skills. Understanding the customer will help you develop a story, and that story will help you repurpose your dream to start a company.

> We promise to pinpoint the problem, tailor the treatment to
> the specific patient, and avoid collateral tissue damage.

In the beginning, we started with one industrial designer and me. Our story was that he and I would design instruments and devices I felt would work best in the surgeon's hands, devices that would require the least invasive surgery, allowing the patient to recover very quickly. We believed that patients experienced hospitals as cold and impersonal and that there were too many risks for infections and other complications. This drove us to develop the Less Exposure Surgery philosophy, which became the story of doing surgeries as outpatient in a surgery center, having patients recover at home. It became a story about less risky techniques and a quick return to the individual patient's lifestyle.

We kept trying to find the best way to tell our story to our customers. Today, our LES story talks about three commitments: we promise to pinpoint the problem, tailor the treatment to the specific patient, and avoid collateral tissue damage. We are about performing less invasive surgery. It is about our KISS principle, to keep it simple and sensible. It is a promise our customers can count on, and it is what has developed the LESS Institute and SpineFrontier into multimillion-dollar companies.

We take listening to our customers to such a degree that we even changed the name of our practice from the earlier name, the Institute for Minimally Invasive Surgery, to the Institute for Modern and Innovative Surgery (iMISSurgery). How did this happen? One of my customers felt "minimal" and "invasive" did not go together. Plus, being that I was a Harvard-trained surgeon, he expected "maximum surgery." We later changed the name to the Less Exposure Surgery Specialists Institute (LESS Institute) to convey the message we avoid doing any more surgery than is needed to treat the problem, avoiding collateral damage commonly seen in today's surgery.

Listening to customers is also why we invested in SenseDriver Technologies for safer driving. It is how we realized patients want to get their diagnoses and information about their physicians online, so we started LESS Institute Online, which morphed into

Mediconnects. All our portfolio companies are about satisfying the consumer above all else. How amazing to have your customers tell you which businesses to start, because you listen to their needs.

I have learned to think more like our customer base than like a businessperson, to avoid focusing too much on operations. Of course, you need to understand how to run a business. But I assure you, if you understand how your customers think and spend every day with them, you will develop a road map of the street smarts required to build a successful business.

I don't believe you can learn to truly service your customers in a classroom, for example by earning your MBA, over spending time with your customers and having the ambition to succeed. You will learn on the job; your employees and customers will be your teachers.

In all our companies, we use the following test to decide what we do that could affect the customer experience: when my employees assess a product or service, instead of asking, "Would the customer like it?" they ask, "Can I see myself as a customer who would like it?" It changes the way we approach product development, because we're not just thinking like the customer; we think of ourselves as the customer, but we get to develop a solution to the customer problem. We are constantly testing our ideas this way; we compare our products to those of our competitors to see trends and understand what is working and not working.

It is also important to treat your customer with patience and honesty. There will be times when you fall short; it happens. But rather than make up excuses, tell your customer the truth and seek a solution to their problem. The sting of an unhappy customer is a gift to spur you into action to improve or innovate, not to be defensive and blame the customer. This needs to be done quickly so the customer feels appreciated and well served by your company.

Every company has these moments; some have to close their doors. But what will set you apart from the competition is how you handle the situation when a mistake happens. Put the customer first and allow their feedback to help you strategize ways in which you can prevent future mistakes. Be accommodating and don't shift blame for your inadequacies; treat them with the respect and courtesy they deserve. Remember that without their support, you will most likely lose the support of others.

> The sting of an unhappy customer is a gift to
> spur you into action to improve or innovate, not
> to be defensive and blame the customer.

When dealing with customers, good communication is priceless. As the head of the company, customers see you as the ultimate solution when a problem arises. If you are not a great communicator, then actively listen and empathize. This is not the time to argue about who is right or wrong; you will only dig a deeper hole. Definitely do not lose your cool. A single customer who feels slighted will do more damage than one hundred happy customers will help you. Unhappy customers will be motivated to hurt you or your business by talking to anyone they can; they'll use any means possible to get back the power you took from them. In today's internet culture, that means the entire world will know they are unhappy with your business.

If you are not a people person, start working on being nicer, and you will learn. If you find someone better than you at working with customers, hire them as soon as possible, but don't hide from your customers. If you are not in touch with your customers regularly in some form, bad things will happen. My team talks about a web of influence, whereby more than one of our employees should be contacting the customer, so the customer has a relationship with many people, increasing the chance of them feeling connected at all times.

Treat customer service like you want to one day win an award for customer service. This needs to be a clear message, that the executive leadership believes customer service is important and invests in the people who have the expertise to develop the strategies to satisfy the customer, as well as measure how well we do so opportunities for improvement will not be missed. I want to make sure we have the focus and resources in place, so that if we think of any way to make the customer experience complete, we do so, not sit there and wonder about it. Then we want to repeat the experience over and over, successfully and without glitches.

Our customer service experience should be like an assembly line, where you break up the experience into steps and think about every detail, all the way to the finished product, leaving no step unaccounted for. I want us to walk our team through each step, get their feedback, and train them until it happens the same way every time, like clockwork. With a sales process, you can identify where in the process you failed with a customer, and maybe you can get someone else to take over from that step, or maybe you get a second chance to correct the steps you last failed at, but you know the steps to follow. A process makes coaching and training the sales team repeatable, so your business builds consistency. Customers might even love to hear about your process and can anticipate and hold your sales team accountable to the process.

Below are the original seven steps we use in our customer experience process to build a relationship that will lead to recurring sales:

1. Understand the customer needs (Discovery).
2. Consult and collaborate (Phone call and in person).
3. Set synergistic milestones (Get the customer to commit).
4. Assign and communicate responsibilities.
5. Analyze process.
6. Commit to customer-customized calendar.
7. Provide ongoing support.

We established a client service center of excellence at our headquarters in Boston, Massachusetts for our clients to visit and have a focused experience. This is similar to the Apple stores you see in the malls. Customers come to our company and see the products on display, and they can touch and feel the products and ask questions to compare with the competition. We get feedback directly from the customers. We need to anticipate what can go wrong and pay special attention to those at-risk steps. In the end, we are all customers, so we use our personal customer experience to refine our own company's customer service but use opportunities to test directly with the customers. We also recently established a customer service group in Kingston Jamaica consisting of lead generator, lead nurturer and scheduler. This team reaches out to new doctors to use our products, nurture the new leads and work closely with the support staff within each dotor's practice to get their surgery schedules so our sales team can provide support.

CONVERT CUSTOMERS INTO CONSUMERS AND BUYERS

So how do we convert the customer into a consumer or buyer?
Converting a customer requires persuasion and influence.

Getting customers usually requires promotion and marketing. I break down promotion into three C's: content, context and conversion. Majority of our promotions today happens on social media. So we tailor our message content to the context of social media and our targeted customer and measure the conversion by how many doctors enter our sales process and become users.

Once you make contact with a potential consumer or buyer, you have a customer that persuaded him or herself or wants to be persuaded by the seller that they are making the right decision. They want to feel satisfied with their purchase. You have likely been in a situation where you are turned off by a business you were ready to buy from; you met a salesperson who you just did not like, so you walked away. You also may enter the business, seeking information on the product, and the salesperson seemed uninformed, so you ask for a manager, who you trust as the authority. You expect that person to know the answers, and if they do not, you lose trust and walk away. How about walking in and getting different answers from three different employees for the same question? You value consistency, and you feel that there was no consistency in the answers; you conclude not to commit and buy anything or come back to the store. Had they given you consistent answers, this would have aligned and consistent with your belief system, and you would have committed to buying that day and likely would have kept coming back.

Denzel Washington repeatedly says that without commitment, you will not start, and without consistency, you will not finish. This is his belief system, so if you want to persuade Denzel, show these characteristics which makes him consistently attracted to those who value consistency and commitment. What if you walked into the store, and at the door they gave you a raffle ticket that said you could redeem it at the cashier after you paid for an item, and if you won, you got a free television? You like to play the lottery and you like to win, so you take the raffle ticket. This is a way to get you to commit to buying because you want to win a television. Now if each time you go to the store, there is some kind of promotion to give you the chance to win, or if you won once, you might become committed to that store and go there consistently. You are consistent in gambling so you will likely play the lottery.

How about being ready to buy, and you ask for a discount or a bag for the product, and they tell you no, to take it or leave it—they don't offer any discounts or give away bags. You leave because it feels like they want your money and did not reciprocate and give you anything you asked for. You decide to not buy the product or go back for another purchase.

Next time, you finish eating at a restaurant and notice the waiter brings you a mint or two with the bill. That act of kindness has been studied to show that you are more likely to add a larger tip than if you were not given a mint. Two mints increase the tip more than a single mint. How about you walk in and notice that there are only four of the products you want to buy, and you just came from two other locations that ran out, so you know you are lucky to see these four? This item is scarce, so you buy all four. I had this experience during the COVID-19 pandemic with toilet tissues. Lastly, you walk in, and there is a long line for a product. You ask why there is a line, and each person says they are buying the latest product that is ecofriendly and it is flying off the shelves. You are big into saving the environment and want to do what you can to contribute to society, so you decide to buy the product. This was our first experience with the Tesla Model X when a friend of ours in Houston told us about his black Model X that he had to wait for almost a year to get. When he explained the features and how it was going to save us from buying gasoline, we had to go buy one. This was enough social proof for us plus he owned a Model X so there was a sense that people will be buying these cars hence the sense of concensus. All these scenarios could be categorized into one or more of Cialdini's six principles of influence, in order:

1. Liking
2. Authority
3. Consistency/commitment
4. Reciprocity
5. Scarcity
6. Consensus/Social proof

This list was introduced in 1984 by Dr. Robert B. Cialdini in his book titled *Influence: The Psychology of Persuasion*. I recommend you buy this book, read it, and keep it close as a refresher. Practice these six tools of influence until you live your life by them, without the need to read them anymore. Before you use these tools, first connect emotionally with the customer. In the perfect case, you have time to research the customer. If not, try to learn about the customer by engaging in conversation and ask questions. Give information about yourself as you reciprocate information you get from the customer to find that emotional space where you can bond. It might be around your children, interests, or sports, but make it happen naturally. It is better to be memorable for being a nice person than for not, so don't let the drive for a sale get ahead of your desire to first bond with someone. Even if the sales cycle may be immediate or you lose the customer, engage to connect using the tools if you must, without being in a rush to persuade. Getting that first impression is immediate, and if it is not good, none of the influence tools will work. Be reminded customers prefer to buy from people they like and respect. The six tools work because they focus you on attending to the customer, which means you are probably going to be likable and respected for showing respect to the customer's needs.

So how do you close the sale? Use the assumed sale technique where you change from persuasion to a process where you are talking past the sale to talk about payment method and continued service for the product and what the after-sale experiences may be. I learned this from my experience buying a car. The salesperson invited the financial guy over to meet me, and then he brought me over to his office and started to ask me how I was going to pay for the car and proceeded to discuss loans and servicing. At this point, I was getting information beyond the sale. Have you noticed when you are buying a house, the Realtor will start talking about what you could do with each room when you live in the house to create the visual beyond the sale. The assumed sale is not a persuasion technique but the way in which you close. In the medical device business, we train the doctor on the product in a cadaver to create the experience of doing the surgery before the actual surgery. This leads to anticipation of using the product. We then leave the product and instruments to be sterilized so the doctor can use it again. Satisfying the customer is the purpose of your business. Never forget this, or the penalty is bankruptcy. There is no point to a business without customers.

How do you treat your customers? Share with us.

QUICK RECAP

Lessons on the Customer:

1. Without the customer, there is no business.
2. Every successful business thrives on satisfying the customer.
3. Sell to your customer's wants and needs every step of the way.
4. Don't oversell what you can deliver.
5. Take time to get to know your customer to connect emotionally.
6. Use the six tools of persuasion.
7. Put yourself in your customer's shoes.
8. Establish a sales process with steps to follow.
9. Remember that a slighted customer can do much damage.
10. Be accessible to your customer.

CHAPTER 11
ESSENTIAL KEY #11

AVOID PRIDE; IT GUARANTEES FAILURE

> Pride in any form clouds your judgment and is only a
> thin veil hiding insecurities. Manifested pride is always
> a sign to watch for, as it is a prodrome for a fall.

Pride is included in this book because it is a trait that can, on one hand, be used positively to drive our desire to prove ourselves, but it can also be a negative force in our personal and business decisions. Pride can bankrupt us in both life and business, blocking our success. The word is often used in a positive way to describe the sense of ownership people feel in their work, meaning they really want their work to be well done and admired. It is used negatively to describe people who think too highly of themselves, to the point of being conceited. These are people who feel they are always right. It is their way or the highway. They would rather fail than move quickly to get the needed help or make the tough decisions, for fear it might appear that they're in trouble.

You may think the first description is a good thing in business, while the latter description refers to someone you should not do business with. No, no, no. I would rather that you completely avoid any definition of pride in reference to people or business, because pride in any form clouds your judgment and is only a thin veil hiding insecurities. Manifested pride is always a sign to watch for, as it is a prodrome for a fall. Always.

How do we learn to manage pride? To manage pride in your life, start by detaching from the material things you own. Avoid feeling the need to fit in with the Joneses to show how successful you are and what you have materially that signals success. Avoid reacting to defend your views as right or retaliating when attacked for whatever reason. Strive to seek knowledge at all times, to stay humble and maintain an insatiable drive to be better at everything you do. These are the very same traits you need to be successful, and this is why pride and success are always at odds. Titles and awards are things to put on your résumé, not to wear around your neck. If you are given them, pay attention to how they help you versus how they weigh you down. For some people, awards and recognition are chains around their neck, worn for everyone else to see, yet many of these awards were applied for, versus rewarded for actual achievement.

> If you pay attention to the world and the people around
> you, you will see the lessons of failed pride everywhere.

I don't apply for awards for this very reason, because if I win the award, there's no consideration of those who did not apply. Because of the award, their actions must fit a certain code of conduct that only they truly value and believe everyone else should value too, hence the constant reminder. They never take the chain off to relax or make an exception in any scenario or move on to bigger and better things, to a different level, where the award is in the past. I am proud of my ten years at Harvard, but I need to be judged on who I am today and what I am accomplishing, not keep celebrating my Harvard degrees.

If you pay attention to the world and the people around you, you will see the lessons of failed pride everywhere. If you are affected by what people think of you, then your decisions will be clouded by pride. We are just passing through this life, and whatever you hold onto will be something you must let go of at some point, so why own it? We were born naked, the same as everyone else, and not of our choosing, and all we have is a ticking clock and health. We were given a healthy brain and body to use, to do something with the time we have. Everything else that we hold onto can weigh us down and limit us from reaching our greatest potential.

I got into my teens and started to feel like a man. My mom used to tell me that she brought me into this world naked, cleaned, fed, clothed me, and gave me shelter, so I better respect her and not be too full of myself. Later, she would say that every tub has to stand on its own feet, instilling in me the confidence to be self-sufficient. If you desire all the objects of success, enjoy them to your heart's content, but don't let material things, titles, memberships, and awards affect your senses or, even worse, make you miss valuable opportunities to succeed even further. We should enjoy the beautiful car because of its attributes, not because of how it makes us look or how it defines our success.

In fact, I am prepared to give it away to someone who might deserve it in my eyes, like an employee who is very valuable to our success. I once gave away a beautiful designer shirt to my date, because she really liked the shirt. She was surprised, but I insisted. Plus, I was a freshman in college at the time and was acting on my true instincts. I later realized that I easily lose my head to beautiful and smart women.

> When it comes to our attitude about material things, we must put people before ourselves and before things—always.

It always amazes me that the more money some people get, the more they try to keep for themselves, or the more success they have in their field, the more self-absorbed they become, even though their position might provide them an outlet to reach and influence more people in a positive way. The more success some people get, the more they feel compelled to let everyone know that what they are doing is important, and they cannot risk taking any chances. What they are saying is they already have success, so there is no real interest in opening themselves up to anything new, unless it's on their terms. Sometimes I daydream about the simpler days, when I had much less money. I was hungry to learn, and I spent more time enjoying the simple pleasures. It was a time before I became more successful and had copious responsibility.

I do, however, enjoy the increased knowledge and wisdom that I have gained over time, and I am still learning. Be smart and wake up to the reality that the lifestyle choices afforded by money are much better than not having money, but when we have success and money, we need to continue to be hungry and act as a sponge, learning from all other people and paying attention to market changes and new innovations. I maintain my hunger and drive by reinvesting my money into more business ventures and constantly setting larger visions. In many ways, I am glad I did not grow up with an excessive amount of money, which would dull my drive and give me a sense that I have enough money and can just take it easy. When it comes to our attitude about material things, we must put people before ourselves and before things—always.

THERE BUT FOR THE GRACE OF GOD GO I

Another practice is to look at ourselves as lucky to be alive and healthy each day. Time and health are two things we cannot control 100 percent, and pride loves control. Be thankful that we don't have a disability, or if we have a disability, think of those who have it worse through no fault of their own. Sometimes I watch a program on television about other people living in humble places. I think, *There but for the grace of God go I*. You don't control when, where, or to whom you are born, so if you recognize that you are lucky to be alive, and if you have good health, you should make use of your good fortune to make a mark in this world. And if nothing else, be nice and helpful to everyone if you can.

If you have the ability, it's probably time for you to consider starting a business and employing people to help them help their family. Don't make your life just about you. We can ask ourselves, "Are we here on earth only to have an easy life and do as little as we can to make a living? What is our purpose?" Think about the things we enjoy and learn about why they exist in the first place. If we do this, we will find that people before us sacrificed for us to enjoy the things that make our lives comfortable. I miss my grandmother so much because she died before I could really thank her enough for all her sacrifices. I wish she could have been at my medical school graduation to share my success and hold my degree.

Understanding the fragility of life reminds me to always stay humble. Is it that hard for us to consider giving something back to the world? To give something for the children behind us to enjoy, the way people before did for us? As I get older, it is clear to me that if I only focused on enjoying time off and doing nothing, I would be wasting my life and taking up someone else's space. So I integrate my happiness into every activity—work, home, or play—and try to contribute meaningfully and improve others' lives through my work.

You might ask, "If you don't have pride, how do you motivate yourself to do well?" With pride as your motivation, you are saying, "I cannot afford to fail. I need to look good. I have to impress people." This would not have motivated me to work for years to achieve success, or if it had, it would have only motivated me for a short time. This kind of thinking means you are not going to take risks, because you might fail. If you fail, you might fall apart or never get back up out of shame. Or you might take too great a risk because you are full of yourself and feel you cannot fail, so you need to have some spectacular success.

Failure is essential for great success; it is the way we get better, the way we are compelled to look for answers and chart a new course. I have no pride in anything I do. I just want to keep reaching to higher levels. I want to be part of a bigger game, with people who are highly successful, not because I want people to admire me or validate what I do but because I want to keep trying to get better.

If we have pride in our lives, we may be afraid to go out and expose ourselves to failure by starting a business, or we may think too big because we want to be famous, or we may want to be different just to be noticed. To grow any company, you need financial investors. The people you know in your life circle are your first source of investment. Not all of them will invest, but you better be prepared to ask all of them, even your enemy. I have had to do this, so I know. If I was afraid to ask because of rejection, I'd be prevented from even asking the people who want to help.

This fear of rejection is planted alongside pride. Each rejection is an opportunity to learn to strengthen your resolve and to keep trying and improving. The bottom line is that pride may make you start thinking about what happens if you fail. Pride may result in second-guessing your actions and thinking about what could go wrong. It can make you think about how you look to others in a clique or to those in membership clubs and societies. Our self-consciousness will start to become a protective shield. We will resist being challenged, and instead, we will focus on how to defend our position. We will shy away from any new opportunity because there is a sense of risk to our current image or title. We will lose the ability to connect and communicate with our employees on an equal level, which is essential for them to buy into our vision. If you need to win every discussion, discussions will become arguments.

All these negatives stem from having pride, so avoid it. People trust you when you connect with them, and that means not hiding your limitations. Be mindful of creating an image of perfection. You will need help to succeed and rise. You will need money to grow your company, so open up and tell your story to investors, and if they don't have money, ask them for their honest feedback on how you can improve your pitch. Your vulnerabilities show you need a team, and everyone on the team is important to its success. Don't make your team feel that this is only your show or that this is all about you having the spotlight. Be a humble student of success who is always seeking knowledge, and learn to fail fast and keep trying, even when people laugh at your failures or write you off.

Some of us walk around trying to pose like a mountain. If you are seen as immovable, blocking the sun and overshadowing everyone around you, it is time to consider being more like a valley. A valley is always ready to receive and grow. The nourishing rain that falls on the mountain flows down to the valley, bringing with it life and growth. The valley flourishes despite being hidden between the mountains. If you try to stand tall, above everyone else, you will be seen, but you will not receive as much, and your head will be exposed to the elements at all times. If you choose to operate as a mountain and not a valley, you will lose out on more than you gain.

Replace pride with humility. Humility is a wonderful thing. Not only does it give you peace and confidence with the people around you, but it also enables you to give up the façade of knowing everything. It allows you to be a constant learner, to always soak up the knowledge of those surrounding you. Humility and lack of pride make it harder for your enemies to destroy you by attacking your pride. I have overcome strategies to publicly humiliate me because I cultivate a lack of shame, As the CEO you put your company at risk if you are affected by what is written and said about you by others. Your humility and integrity should be unshakeable and not be based on how you are judged, By avoiding feeling pride you will avoid making decisions based on pride. By approaching your company with humility, you set yourself up to receive information from everyone, whether they are the executive officers in your company, customers, or the janitorial staff. It makes the company about more than just you; it opens the business up to achieving a greater purpose. It will aid in your innovation process. And because you trust and support your people to do their jobs and you make yourself available, you allow their skills to benefit the greater purpose of the company. This ensures that your whole company can be a fertile, growing valley.

What is your experience with pride? Share with us..

QUICK RECAP

Lessons on Pride:

1. Pride and jealousy are roommates; avoid both.
2. Pride clouds your judgment, hides insecurities, and comes before a fall.
3. To rid yourself of pride, begin by detaching from the material things you acquire.
4. Enjoy the lifestyle of success and appreciate the objects success breeds. But remember, it's better to share them with others than to have things just for you to say you have them. Pass away fulfilled and rich, not rich and unfulfilled.
5. Realize you are lucky to be alive and to have your health. This is reason enough to give back.
6. Pride leaves you concerned with what others think and makes you afraid of failure. This fear ultimately makes you avoid new opportunities to work with others.
7. Sharing your vulnerabilities with people will help them trust you.
8. Be a valley and not a mountain.
9. Replace your pride with humility.
10. Humility allows you to be a constant learner and to soak up others' knowledge.

CHAPTER 12
ESSENTIAL KEY #12
CHOOSE TO SUCCEED

There is nothing more beneficial to the progress of humankind than those people who choose to have a strong will to succeed.

So you've decided to prove yourself, but have you looked in the mirror and humbly acknowledged your true situation? If yes, your next step is to tell yourself, "I am going to achieve great success, prove myself, and find a way, no matter what or how long it will take." You must make a conscious decision to succeed. It's not enough to just try to evade failure.

Success is a result of the habits you practice and the discipline you have in learning and making adjustments while you persevere. Growing up, my mother made sure I went to church every Sunday, rain or shine. If I complained and tried to avoid it, she would simply say, "You are going." There was a time when I also went to the Seventh-day Adventist church, and it was the same diligence every Friday to Saturday evening. To this day, if I go to bed without praying, I feel guilty, like I just dissed God and need to make it up. This is an example of habit forming.

Religion is a healthy habit that helps you develop inner restraint so you pause to consider, "Is this the right thing to do?" Especially if there is a possibility that you could break the law or hurt someone, the inner voice that religion gives you could save you from failure or prison or, even worse, untimely death. I have learned that success does not have to be achieved through cheating or hurting people; success is more likely when you play fair and square and abide by the rules through hard work, resourcefulness, and street smarts. I also learned that the universe will help you when you truly believe in achieving something great and work toward your goal. Many times, I have proven this to be true, so I am always a believer in whatever I set out to do; otherwise, I don't begin with it.

Success for me started early in my life. As a child, I was dirt poor, and once I realized that my father had left and was never coming back, I made the choice to succeed financially, to become a leader, and to be an example to others. I had plenty of negative motivation around me in lifestyles of poverty, drinking, smoking, and so on that I saw destroy people. But I also had positive motivators, like my best friend's family circumstances and how they lived. I first saw the objects of their success: the two cars, the multiple-bedroom house, the well-stocked refrigerator, the summer trips to America, nice clothes, and what seemed like a worry-free lifestyle. I wanted this lifestyle.

So once I made the choice to succeed, it affected how I approached all my actions; no matter how small, I only wanted to do things that were going to prepare me to succeed. I wanted to focus on education and being an eternal learner, to soak in information from everyone about success. When I heard you need to be a great student to build the foundation for success, I became one. When I heard that businessmen and doctors and lawyers do well financially, I put those professions on my list. When I heard that athletes did well too, I took athletics to the next level; I played soccer and every other sport that was offered every day. My friends would call me "Competition" because in everything I did, I wanted to be the best.

I was always trying to start a contest with the simplest things.

When I was eight or nine, I remember a neighbor had a business selling these frozen syrup drinks, called "suck suck" in Jamaica. I took my batch to school and sold them all during recess. I was out in the school yard, selling those things quickly. I don't remember how much I got paid, but I remember how it felt to be selling and getting customers to buy. The point is I was not born with success on my mind, nor do I recall any specific moment that my destiny appeared to me. I made the choice because of my circumstances. I wanted to succeed for many reasons, but what mattered most was that I made the choice to succeed, and I continue to renew that choice every day, because success is about improving yourself, setting new goals, and achieving them.

> I wanted to succeed for many reasons, but what mattered
> was that I made the choice to succeed, and I continue
> to renew that choice every day, because success is about
> improving yourself, setting new goals, and achieving them.

SUCCESS IS YOUR GIFT TO YOURSELF AND HUMANITY

When I hear people discuss success, the conclusion is usually that it's an individual concept and that if people think they are successful, then it's fine for them to feel that way. I am fortunate no one tried to sell me on this self-serving copout when I was an impressionable young boy. I am glad there were teachers who pushed me to get better grades and to set lofty goals and work hard to achieve them, rather than settling on thinking success is whatever I define it to be. It is true that you must define your own goals, and if you achieve them, you'll most likely feel that tinge of success. I define five categories to measure your success: happiness, wealth, health, a sense of life meaning, and gratitude. These are the five areas I think of every day to try to achieve work-life balance. I'm grateful I started companies to employ people, so they can take care of their families and I can take care of mine, rather than tell myself I am successful just because I say so.

I tell myself I am not yet successful, so I keep setting bigger goals and keep working toward them; in the end, I just want to keep progressing to become the best person I can be. The day I am convinced I am successful is the day I effectively start a new journey to fail, because if you are not trying to succeed, then you are trying to avoid failure. Can you imagine a world where everyone thinks success is merely personal? We would still be in the Dark Ages because we would all be fine with our situation, telling ourselves all is cool and there's no need to work too hard. People were given a will, and there is nothing stronger than the will to succeed and improve our lives. There is nothing more beneficial to the progress of humankind than those people who choose to have a strong will to succeed. These are the people who make the world a better place for the rest.

How do you choose to succeed? You can do this at any stage of your life. But the earlier, the better, because to succeed, you need time and small wins along the way to boost your confidence. In this book, we talked about studying other successful people and transforming yourself to overcome your weaknesses.

You must choose to succeed, or you are by default choosing to fail. If you do not continuously place goals in front of you and decide to apply a strong will to achieve them, you will forever be working to keep yourself from failing rather than succeeding. People who choose to cruise never feel they are deciding to fail; it's just a fact that is lost on them. We are all just one bad decision or one unfortunate mishap from financial disaster, so how can you cruise though life just doing enough? Would you blame your friends if you made the choice to delay work to spend time hanging out, then found yourself without a job because you missed a deadline or completed the task sloppily due to lack of dedication? If your boss gives you a lot of space to be self-driven and your company has high expectations for you, but instead you abuse it to waste time or not live up to expectations, you will find yourself fired and without opportunity to succeed.

This book emphasizes financial success. With financial success, all things become possible. Money will factor in every major decision you make. Money is the currency for valuing things in every advanced society; you need to have money to live and to change people's lives and the world around you. I believe if you have health, you should develop the will to succeed financially, to go as high as you can, to reap the lifestyle benefits of success, and to help others learn how to succeed. If we all did this, the world would improve for everyone.

I choose to affect the world directly through achieving personal financial success and learning enough so that I can become a teacher and mentor my employees. With my financial success building companies, I can develop innovative products for consumers to improve their lives, and with financial success comes the opportunity for philanthropy. I would like to create a sustainable philanthropic foundation that can be funded by private monies from my companies, with contributions from other successful entrepreneurs. My greatest legacy (besides being a good father to my children) would be establishing a KICVentures company in every major city of the world and providing funding and knowledge to budding entrepreneurs. It is through supporting other entrepreneurs that I can have the broadest impact on changing the world, rather than through any direct philanthropy with my own money. What use is it to give a man a fish? The next day, he will need another. Long-term, sustainable philanthropy comes from teaching people to fish, by providing knowledge and support to grow businesses.

> With financial success comes the
> opportunity for philanthropy.

I feel saddened when the richest people do not show a strong desire to engage and help other budding entrepreneurs. Ironically, it's a missed opportunity, since they spent their lives growing money but are not passing their knowledge down to aspiring entrepreneurs. Imagine how many great ideas for improving the world languish among driven, young people who, unless they have the right connections or pedigree, are destined to fail because they lack the mentorship and funding. Only the very lucky few, who find luck of circumstance and timing, get funding to grow their businesses or succeed after receiving money from angel investors. But these angel investors come along, and after undervaluing the business, they can take the majority of it.

Bob Marley said, "Who the cap fit, let them wear it." So I am challenging those who succeed to look down the ladder and find ways to use money to fund other entrepreneurs more openly and establish mentorship opportunities. This might be the most rewarding philanthropic experience because you live creatively through others, who can benefit from your money and expertise. There is no finish line to this approach, as it is propagated from generation to generation, and each new generation designates portions of their wealth to help others.

You must make the choice to succeed.

If you don't choose to succeed, you will not be able to take advantage of the lessons in this book; in fact, that is one of the reasons we chose to make this the final chapter, so you would be left with the reminder that you must make the choice to succeed.

Without making that choice, no amount of advice or encouragement will make success happen in your life. It is not something that magically happens. It is not free; success must be earned. It is something that must be strived for from within, and it can only be attained by the act of full-heartedly chasing it, being 100 percent all in. Many people want success, but only those who choose to develop the necessary will to succeed at all costs achieve it; they open their hearts to learn how to succeed.

ROADBLOCKS TO CHOOSING SUCCESS

People are often more afraid of the work it takes to succeed than of failure. Likewise, they fear the work it takes to manage success versus simply settling on being average. Success requires a big commitment, and some would argue it requires too much time, work, and suffering through growing pains to be worth it. For this reason, many are content to stay below the radar, to live the status quo life, to fit into the crowd and never rise to their full potential. Make no mistake, this is choosing to fail. You might not see yourself as failing if you have evaded failure so far. People who choose to fail but don't realize they made that choice are the same ones avoiding significant dedication to their work. They are the ones who really work three days per week (Tuesday, Wednesday, and Thursday) because to them, Monday is a day of catchup, and Friday is for thinking about the weekend. I implore my team to use Fridays to close out what they were working on during the week and plan for the next week, so they are really working Monday through Thursday, and Friday is close-out day. I don't expect my team to work on weekends. That is why they don't start companies, and I understand. I plan work for me to do over the weekend, and I use that time to plan what I need other people to do the following week. That way, they can hit the ground running on Monday, while I have less to do and can devote my time to supervising.

Ask yourself, can you afford to be sick and not work for a year? Can you help someone take care of their family by offering them a job? These are two questions for which you need clear answers, answers that can help you choose to succeed. It does not mean you need to start your own company, but that is an option to consider strongly. Start by being around successful people and approach your work with success in mind, as if you own the company. If you do, I expect your boss will want to help ensure that you succeed, because for a company to prosper, it needs people focused on success. How many times have you heard of someone cashing out of their start-up company and living a life of luxury? These are people who chose to succeed, joined others with the same mindset, and dedicated the time and effort to build equity. You don't have to be the boss; you just need to make the choice to succeed in the position you're in and have a strong will to do so.

People who feel success is whatever they decide it to be personally often try to equate success with unhappiness. They say that working too hard means you don't spend time with your loved ones and your friends, or that success and money turn a person into someone they don't want to become. It's easy for them to write off the objects of success and say, "I don't need those things; therefore, success is not something I want to chase."

PROVE YOURSELF BY CHOOSING SUCCESS

Rather than focusing on the objects of success, get closer to the lifestyle of it, the freedom of choice, the ability to help other people, the opportunity to enjoy life on your time and terms. The objects of success do not on their own make someone happy; I agree. But unless you have had a lot of money, try not to dismiss someone who does, because you just don't know what it feels like to have financial success until you have it.

You will do things you never thought
you were capable of doing.

You will realize that throughout your journey, after you have chosen to succeed and taken steps toward reaching your fullest God-given potential, there is not a specific endpoint.

You will do things you never thought you were capable of doing. You will learn how to identify your passion and pursue it; you will discover how to work hard and smart; you will know how to work effectively with a team; you will make money; you will manage your time; you will care about other people; you will navigate the ebb and flow of life; you will look to others; you will overcome failure; you will practice humility; and you will learn something new every step of the way. This is what success looks like and why it's worth all the effort.

Proving yourself through success opens the door to opportunity. It gives you the chance to live a life of continued growth and reward. It gives you financial freedom and the independence to spend time on your terms. 'Nuff said. Let's get to it; get started with your desire to succeed and turn up your game.

What are you choosing to succeed at? Share with us.

QUICK RECAP

Choose to Succeed:

1. You must make a conscious decision to succeed.
2. Making the choice to succeed affects everything you subsequently do.
3. People who say success is what they decide it to be are afraid to try to succeed.
4. You can choose to succeed at any stage of life, and small wins will boost your confidence.
5. Choosing to cruise is the acceptance of failure.

6. The will for financial success changes your life and others' lives for the better.

7. Once you succeed, you can help others do the same, and the world will be a better place.

8. Success requires commitment, work, suffering, and time, but being afraid of this is choosing to give up.

9. Success isn't about the objects of success as much as it's about the lifestyle and financial freedom.

10. Proving yourself through success gives you opportunity and lets you live a life of continued growth and reward.

It's not about where you start; it's where you end up.

BIBLIOGRAPHY

The Holy Bible, New International Version (Grand Rapids, MI: Zondervan, 1984).

ABOUT THE AUTHOR

Dr Kingsley R Chin is a doctorpreneur honors graduate of Harvard Medical School, Harvard Business School in leadership and Columbia College and Engineering. He is an orthopedic spine-surgeon professor and founder-ceo of KIC healthcare-investment company since 2004. He builds KIC Ventures as an institutional legacy supporting business leadership. Born poor in Buff Bay Portland Jamaica to a teenage mother he is relentless to impact and influence people through leadership, books, speeches and entrepreneurship.

My vision pulls me along and fuels my desire to continuously educate myself on how to succeed in life and business, to rise far above the low level that I started out at in life. How does my vision continue to drive me even though I have risen to much success? I have made it a habit to pursue success and to not become comfortable with past successes. The way you get success is from success, no matter how small. So I am always working on success, and as I achieve successes, I am able to see more opportunities to succeed. Daily, I look myself in the mirror to remind myself I am underachieving, and I must keep learning and staying relevant in the world today so I can make an impact and be influential. I know I can achieve more because when I compare what I know today versus a few months ago or a year ago, I see that I could have done better in the past if I had the knowledge I have today. You also don't know what you don't know you don't know, so I want to learn fast so I can achieve more. Achieving more is not just a quantity; for me, it is being able to win trophies and close out many of my opportunities.

Printed in the United States
by Baker & Taylor Publisher Services